KW-480-383

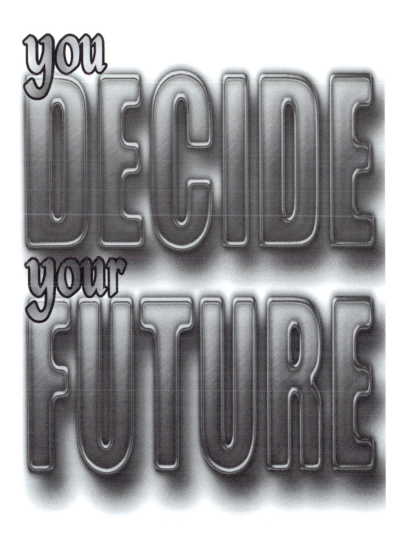

you DECIDE your FUTURE

THOMAS MEARES

Unless otherwise indicated, all Scripture quotations are taken from the King James Version of the Bible.

You Decide Your Future
ISBN 1-931600-21-X
Copyright © 2002 by Thomas Meares

Published by Omega Christian Ministries International
P.O. Box 2745
Lumberton, NC 28359

Printed in the United States of America. All rights reserved under International Copyright law. Contents and /or cover may not be reproduced in whole or in part in any form without prior written consent of the Publisher.

Table Of Contents

Acknowledgements

I have many people to be thankful for in my life. First, I must give honor to the precious Holy Spirit who is my best friend. I could have never written this book without His assistance. Thank you Holy Spirit.

Special thanks to my wife Cathy, who is a wonderful and talented helpmate. I would not be the man I am today without her encouragement and belief in me. Also, thanks to my daughter, Sarah, who is always willing to help her daddy.

There are several great mentors in my life that have greatly influenced me as a minister of the Gospel. I want to thank Dr. Mike Murdock, Author, Songwriter, Evangelist, Teacher and Founder of The Wisdom Center, Denton, Texas, for his tremendous impact on my life. He challenged me several years ago at his School of Ministry to write a book. Having been able to take advantage of the opportunity to be mentored publicly and privately by Dr. Mike Murdock is more valuable than I can explain. Thank you, Dr. Murdock, for continuing to challenge me, and thank you for your valuable mentorship.

Dr. Lyndon Purifoy, Apostle, Pastor, Teacher and Founder of New Covenant School of Ministry, Whiteville, North Carolina, is another great mentor who continues to encourage me to become more. Thank you, Dr. Purifoy, for all the valuable teaching you continue to give me.

I also want to thank my parents, my mother, Jo Ann Meares, for her continued prayers for me and the ministry. My dad, Ertle Ray Meares, (who has gone to be with Jesus) for his Bible teaching and his love for the Word. I am so thankful for the example my Godly parents set for me.

Last but not least, I want to thank all the people involved in helping me write this book. Tonia Olson, for many hours of transcribing. Jenni Dry, for her invaluable help in editing. David & Dora Martin, who did a great job proofing. Daniel Martin at The Increase Group, for a fabulous cover design. All the others, who helped in any capacity. Also, a special thank you for the financial support of Pastor Keith Britt and Family Worship Assembly Church in Coward, South Carolina.

Foreword

Any Book That Unlocks Your Faith Is Invaluable To You.

That's why you need this book.
God *created* the seasons of your life.
Your *Faith* schedules their *timing*.

The Holy Spirit has stirred the heart of Thomas Meares to pen the revelation of his heart to a very needy body of Christ. The Enemy of confusion is Wisdom. This book could change your faith life forever.

Thomas Meares has one of the purest hearts of love I have ever encountered. He has been in my home. He has assisted in many Schools of Wisdom. He is my personal friend. His very countenance truly radiates the joy of Jesus.

He *knows* Faith.
He *lives* Faith.
He *communicates* Faith with passion.

Within this book are Answers. Answers that can dispel depression, calm confusion and every fear you have faced.

It is a joy to commend this book to those serious about a *victorious* life.

Dr. Mike Murdock

Why I Wrote This Book

M any people are in difficult places in their lives. We all have experienced times of anguish, grief and pain. I believe that most of these experiences are the results of our decisions. When we find ourselves in difficult situations, we often want to blame someone or something someone has done. We say it was someone else's fault, someone else made us do it, or people have lied about us. We may blame a history of abuse or a dysfunctional family for our problems. The fact is that our decisions create our circumstances. We can find a path out of adversity by making quality decisions. If people wrong us, we are not to wrong them in return. According to God's Word, we are to return good for evil. (Romans 12:21) Our future will never improve until we accept the fact that our decisions create our future. We are in control of those decisions. That is why it is vitally important for us to accept responsibility for them. God has given us the right to decide, or choose, our future.

In this book, we will look at several things we can do to affect our future. It is not an exhaustive list but if you read these eight chapters with an open mind and prayerful attitude, you will discover that you are more in control of your future than you realized. Your future is in your hands. You decide your future!

Your Choice Is Your Decision

Chapter One

You Decide Your Future By Exercising Your Right To Choose

Y ou have a right to will. Your will is part of your soul. God gave us the right to choose. He gave us the right to will. In the beginning, God spoke the earth into existence, and we know there is power in our words. But just as powerful is our right to will. We choose what we're going to say, and what we're going to think.

There are many places where the Bible uses the word "will" or the phrase "I will." In the New Testament, which originally was written in Greek, the word means "to determine or choose" (Strong's Concordance). The Old Testament translation from Hebrew is "desire" or "pleasure." It is God's will, His desire, or His good pleasure. It is your right to choose, desire, and determine. We can choose good, or we can choose evil; and it is so important that we make the right decisions. God created us with the ability to choose. That's why there will always be choices.

> *"And if it seem evil unto you to serve the Lord,*
> ***choose*** *you this day whom ye* ***will*** *serve; whether*
> *the gods which your fathers served that were on*
> *the other side of the flood, or the gods of the*
> *Amorites, in whose land ye dwell: but as for me*
> *and my house, we* ***will*** *serve the Lord."*
>
> Joshua 24:15

Are you going to serve the gods who were on the other side of the flood? Are you going to serve your past, your failures, and your defeats? Are you going to serve your present – where you are right now? Are you just going to stay there and never move any further? Joshua said, "'as for me and my house, we **will** serve the Lord." He was saying that he and his family were going into the future God had for them. They weren't staying in mediocrity. They knew God had more for them, and they decided to leave the place where they were and possess the inheritance God had promised them.

Let's look at some other scriptures.

> *"Elijah came near to all the people, and said,*
> *How long will you halt and limp* ***between two opin-***
> ***ions?*** *If the Lord is God, follow Him! But if Baal,*
> *then follow him. And the people did not answer*
> *him a word."*
>
> I Kings 18:21 (Amp)

Take notice of the words "between two opinions." Here we see Elijah giving the people a choice, but they would not even make a decision. It is not much different today.

Even when people are given a choice, many will not make a decision.

"Your Choice is Your Decision."

God always gives us choices, but He allows us to make the decision. The following scriptures are an example of our right to choose.

15)   *"See, I have set before thee this day life and good, and death and evil;*
16)   *In that I command thee this day to love the Lord thy God, to walk in His ways, and to keep His commandments and His statutes and His judgments, that thou mayest live and multiply· and the Lord thy God shall bless thee in the land whither thou goest to possess it.*
17)   *But if thine heart turn away, so that thou **wilt** not hear, but shalt be drawn away, and worship other gods, and serve them;*
18)   *I denounce unto you this day, that ye shall surely perish, and that ye shall not prolong your days upon the land, whither thou passest over Jordan to go to possess it.*
19)   *I call heaven and earth to record this day against you, that I have set before you life and death, blessing and cursing: **therefore choose life**, that both thou and thy seed may live:"*
                                        Deuteronomy 30:15-19

I'm not serving my past anymore. I'm not going back to what once was. I'm not going back to the things from which God has delivered me. Paul said to the Galatians,

"Are you foolish? Why are you so foolish that you returned to the things that God has delivered you?" (See Galatians 3:1-5)

You and I decide our own future. You can write your own ticket with God. God has said choose life that you and your seed may live.

God gave you the right to choose, to will. I challenge you today to make the choice to do what God's telling you to do. Make the choice to embrace what God is saying about you. Make the choice to receive the favor and the grace of God upon your life. Allow the divine influence of God to shine upon your heart and be manifested through your life. That's what grace is. I challenge you today to come forth. You have the right to decide your future. God has given you the right to choose whom you will serve.

You decide your future by what you choose, what you will, what you decide. Many times I heard my daddy say something to the effect of "You make the bed hard, you're going to have to lie in it." In other words, the decisions and choices you make determine the outcome of situations, whether they're good or bad. That's why it's so important that you make the right choices.

> **"Your Choice Determines the Outcome Of Your Situation."**

Notice what the book of Isaiah says about the eunuchs.

4) *"For thus saith the Lord unto the eunuchs that keep My sabbaths, and **choose** the things that please Me, and take hold of My covenant;*

5) *Even unto them will I give in Mine house and within My walls a place and a name better than of sons and of daughters: I will give them an everlasting name, that shall not be cut off."*

Isaiah 56:4-5

God said He would give to the eunuchs because they had kept His sabbaths and had chosen the things that pleased Him. They held fast to His covenant. In the same way, we determine, choose, will, or decide our future. Again and again in the Bible, the Lord says, "If you **will** keep My statutes and commandments, I **will** bless you and take care of you." In other words, God's promises and blessings are conditional. They are based on your choice.

You have an obligation to choose. It is your God-given responsibility. You can make wrong choices, and He's not happy about them; but He will allow the outcome based on your decision. Genesis 1:26 and 28 tell us that God gave man dominion. He gave you and me complete authority over the earth. You can make the choice to take the authority that's yours. You can take authority over situations and circumstances and rise above them.

There's a song that asks, "Whose report will you believe?" Then the next line says "We shall believe the report of the Lord." If I get a bad report, I'm going to choose to believe the report of the Lord. I'm not going to accept a physician's bad report. I will accept the diagnosis and not deny what is there. If you have cancer, you have cancer. If you say 97 times or 97,000 times that you don't have cancer, you still have the disease. You have to say, "I rebuke you, devil. By the stripes of Jesus, I am healed. Cancer has no right to be in my body, because I'm a child of God

15

and the body of Christ is not sick." You have to make the choice to say you will have nothing to do with anything that isn't of God. You have to choose what the Word of God says about healing instead of accepting a diagnosis.

I make the choice everyday to give honor, praise, and glory to God. I love on Him every morning, and call Him by the many names that express what He is to me. You see, the different names of God describe what He is to us. When you give honor, praise, and glory to those names and sanctify the name of God, you're saying, "This is what He is to me."

"This is what You are to me, God. I love You. I adore You. I hallow Your name. You are Jehovah-Rapha, the God, my healer, the One who makes bitter experiences sweet, the One who sent His Word and healed me and delivered me from all of my destructions." Not only did Jehovah-Rapha send His Word and heal me. He delivered me from my pit, and my destructions. (Psalm 107:20Amp)

You must understand that you have to make a choice every day to hallow the names of God and what He means to you.

God has so much for you if you'll choose to accept what He has to give. It's your decision to say, "God, I'm going to receive everything You have for me. I'm going to be everything You want me to be. I make the decision. I use my will to submit to Your will and Your plan for my life so I can be a giant in Your Kingdom."

Look at Hebrews 11:24-25.

24) *"By faith Moses, when he was come to years, refused to be called the son of Pharaoh's daughter;* 25) **Choosing** *rather to suffer affliction with the people of God, than to enjoy the pleasures of sin for a season;"*

Moses could have chosen to stay right there and have everything he wanted served to him on a silver platter – servants and everything. He could have continued to identify himself as an Egyptian, even though he discovered who he really was. Moses didn't decide who he was. He discovered who he was - a deliverer. You can do the same thing.

You don't have to be separated from God. You can be joined to Him. You can be like Jesus. However, you have to choose to be like Jesus. You have to decide. "I will be like my elder Brother Jesus. I **will** walk like Him. I **will** talk like Him. I **will** live like Him. I **will** do what He says. I **will** say what He says. I **will** be like Him." It's your choice.

The writer of Psalms 7:17 wrote:

*"I **will** praise the Lord according to his righteousness: and **will** sing praise to the name of the Lord most high."*
Psalms 7:17, emphasis added

You make the choice to praise God, to sing praise to Him. Or you make the choice to be sad and stay under your circumstances. You can choose to let the circumstances be on top of you, or you can choose to be on top of them. Things happen, but you don't have to accept the negative

17

things that happen. Some may say you're living in denial, but it is possible to live in both reality and truth.

I've heard a person say, "Well, I guess I'm going to die of a heart attack when I'm in my fifties. My daddy and my uncle died of a heart attack when they were fifty." You can choose to do that, but guess what? I'm not dying when I'm fifty because I will to walk in health, to live in health, and to have the blessings of God on my life.

You know what the devil does sometimes when you make statements like that? He jumps on your shoulder and says, "You shouldn't be saying all that." Well, phooey on the devil. I'm going to say these things because I have a right to say them. God gave me the will to say what His Word says. And I will have it that way instead of having it the other way.

1) *"I **will** praise Thee, O Lord, with my whole heart; I **will** shew forth all Thy marvellous works.*
2) *I **will** be glad and rejoice in Thee: I **will** sing praise to Thy name, O Thou most High."*
                           Psalms 9:1-2, emphasis added

Do you see that? **I will**. Come hell or high water, I don't care how many things break down, I'm deciding to give God glory and praise, and I'm going to reap the benefits because the Bible says that He inhabits the praises of His people. (Psalm 22:3) When I **will** to praise Him, I know He's going to inhabit me and I'm going to feel strength because of my decision to praise Him no matter what happens. I'm going to say, "Glory to God! I praise You, Lord! I have decided I **will** glorify and praise You, Lord!" I'm not letting circumstances get me down. I've decided to be glad and rejoice in the Lord.

Now, look at Psalm 9, verses nine and ten.

9)   *"The Lord also **will** be a refuge for the op-*
pressed, a refuge in times of trouble.
10)   *And they that know Thy name **will** put their*
trust in Thee: for Thou, Lord, hast not forsaken them
that seek Thee."

Why? Because when you decide to praise, worship, and glorify Him, He's going to be a refuge for you in times of trouble. And that makes me think about Jehovah-Shammah, the God who will never leave or forsake me, a very present help in times of trouble. That's what He is for me. Brothers and sisters, He's Jehovah-Shammah, the God who's always there, no matter what happens.

If you **will** to put your trust in Him — if you **choose** to put your trust in God – He will not forsake you. If you decide to trust Him, you're not going to be forsaken in your future.

Now I'm going to give you some examples of Jesus' **will** in the book of Matthew.

1)   *"When He was come down from the mountain,*
great multitudes followed Him.
2)   *And, behold, there came a leper and worshipped*
*Him, saying, Lord, if Thou **wilt**, Thou canst make*
me clean.
3)   *And Jesus put forth His hand, and touched him,*
*saying, I **will**; be thou clean. And immediately his*
leprosy was cleansed."
                    Matthew 8:1-3, emphasis added

19

I have always loved this scripture. The leper said "if you **will**" and Jesus said "I **will**." His **will** has always been to make us clean. Again, the definition for will is "to wish, desire, delight to, determine, or choose."

- If you *will* . . .
- If you *wish* . . .
- If you *desire* . . .
- If you *delight* in doing it . . .

Jesus **willed**, desired, delighted, determined and chose to make the leper clean. Now look at another example of Jesus' **will**.

> 5) *"And when Jesus was entered into Capernaum, there came unto Him a centurion, beseeching Him,*
> 6) *And saying, Lord, my servant lieth at home sick of the palsy, grievously tormented.*
> 7) *And Jesus saith unto him, I **will** come and heal him."*
>
> Matthew 8:5-7

What happened here? This is a good example of God's **will** to heal anyone. This was a Roman centurion's servant, but Jesus **willed** to heal him.

Jesus **willed** to do something. You have to **will** to do things. If you'll begin to speak the right things and exercise your right to will, things will happen as they did with Jesus. You decide your future by your choice, your will, your decisions, and your determination.

In Matthew chapter 12, even the unclean spirits will to do something. Note the power of **will**.

43) *"When the unclean spirit is gone out of a man, he walketh through dry places, seeking rest, and findeth none.*
44) *Then he saith, I will return into my house from whence I came out; and when he is come, he findeth it empty, swept, and garnished.*
45) *Then goeth he, and taketh with himself seven other spirits more wicked than himself, and they enter in and dwell there: and the last state of that man is worse than the first. Even so shall it be also unto this wicked generation."*

Matthew 12:43-45

Here we see that the unclean spirit had a right to will. He made a decision to go back. Lucifer had a will, a right to choose. He decided he wanted to ascend and be like the Most High. So spirits also have a right to will. That's why it is so important that you exercise your will to kick the devil out, and if he comes back, you will kick him out again. The power of **will** is awesome.

Take, as another example, the rich man in Luke chapter 12.

18) *"And he said, This will I do: I will pull down my barns, and build greater; and there will I bestow all my fruits and my goods.*
19) *And I will say to my soul, Soul, thou hast much goods laid up for many years; take thine ease, eat, drink, and be merry."*

Luke 12:18-19

He decided. He made a choice. But, he made the wrong choice because he trusted himself. He made a god of him-

21

self instead of accepting the true God, and he wound up in hell.

Now let's look at the prodigal son in Luke 15. After he got his share of his inheritance, the prodigal son went on a journey and spent all of his money. He wound up in a pigpen, hungry enough to eat old refuse – the terrible, rotten stuff pigs are fed.

However, when he realized the power of **will**, and his right to make a choice, he made a decision to get out of the pigpen.

18) *"I **will** arise and go to my father, and **will** say unto him, Father, I have sinned against heaven, and before thee,*
19) *And am no more worthy to be called thy son: make me as one of thy hired servants.*
20) *And he arose, and came to his father . . ."*
Luke 15:18-20

You have the right to will, to "arise," to do something about your life. Jesus **willed**. The unclean spirits willed. You have the right to will. You can say I will stay where I am or I will accept the challenge of those who are pushing, prodding, encouraging, and admonishing me. I **will** be everything God has called me to be. I **will** go forth and do the will of the Father. I have the right to choose. I **will** be what God wants me to be. I encourage you to exercise your right to choose. Decide and **will** that you're going to be the person of God that you're supposed to be, and do all that God has said for you to do. Decide to accept what God says about you and be mighty for Him. That's true humility – when you accept what God is saying. ***You Decide Your Future By Exercising Your Right To Choose.***

Notes

You Will Only Rise To The Level Of Your Self-Portrait

Chapter Two

You Decide Your Future
By The Thoughts You Think

It all starts with a thought. It starts with a picture in your mind. Your mind is like an office with two super visors, Mr. Success and Mr. Defeat. You decide whom your mind's going to work for that day. If you decide to work for Mr. Success and you think successful thoughts, you will allow your mind to think on good things, lovely things, and the good report. Or you may get up feeling bad. You think to yourself, "Well, Sister So-And-So has a chip on her shoulder against me. I can just see her now. She's talking about me. She's running me down to the dogs. I'm just going to serve Mr. Defeat." You got up on the wrong side of the bed, and you have a bad picture in your mind. If you have the wrong picture, change it. You need to say "no" to Mr. Defeat and work for Mr. Success, who pays much better wages.

The battlefield is in the mind, and the devil attacks you in your mind. If you have the wrong picture of your future, you need to change it. It's so important that we renew our minds, our thoughts, and what we choose to look at because the Bible says:

*"For as he **thinketh** in his heart, so is he . . ."*
Proverbs 23:7

Your thoughts, and the mental pictures you carry, came from a source. They came from God or from the enemy. The Bible tells us that "as a man thinketh in his heart, so is he."

You decide your future by the thoughts you think. If you think you can . . . you can. If you think you can't . . .you can't. If you think you are defeated . . . you will be defeated. If you think you are victorious . . . you will be victorious.

Man is made up of a body, soul and spirit. First of all, you are spirit and you have a soul, which is your mind, your emotions, and your right to choose (the will). As I said in the previous chapter, you can **will** to do whatever you want to do, because God gave you that right. Likewise God has also given you and me the ability to **think,** which is a function of your mind.

Paul tells us in his letter to the Philippians the things we should think about.

*"Finally, brethren, whatsoever things are true, whatsoever things are honest, whatsoever things are just, whatsoever things are pure, whatsoever things are lovely, whatsoever things are of good report; if there be any virtue, and if there be any praise, **think** on these things."*
Philippians 4:8

The word "brethren" in the beginning of this verse refers to people who are saved. If you've accepted the Lord into your heart, you are saved. Your body and your mind aren't really there yet, but none of us are really there as we should be. All of us must continually renew our mind and subdue our flesh.

Paul listed several types of thoughts. He didn't only say, "Whatsoever things are true, **think** on these things." It may be true that people mistreated me, so that I felt lower than dirt. It might be true that someone I know is lazy and never does anything productive. But Paul didn't stop there. He went on to say:

> "...whatsoever things are _honest,_ whatsoever things are _just,_ whatsoever things are _pure,_ whatsoever things are _lovely,_ whatsoever things are of _good report_..."
>
> Philippians 4:8, emphasis added

It might be true that somebody is lazy. But is it lovely and is it a good report? Is it a good report when you talk about people and their problems? Is it lovely? Is it pure? If it's not, you don't need to think it or say it. It doesn't make it any better if you're willing to say negative things to a person's face. You're still wrong because you're not applying the whole verse and thinking on the right things. You're not looking through the eyes of love. You're not seeing the potential God sees in everyone. God sees things that many times we can't see.

God sees a diamond in the rough sometimes. His gold doesn't always come wrapped in satin. It sometimes comes wrapped in burlap. We have to be willing to mine for the gold. I'm telling you there's gold in them there hills, but you have to be willing to do some digging. Sometimes there's gold in people around us, although that looks impossible from the outside. We have to learn how to reach in there and get the gold. We need to allow the Lord to open our eyes so we can see the potential in others. We really can't know each other unless we know Him.

Sometimes we think we know everything. What really is important is that we have a relationship with God. When we understand Him, we can understand ourselves. You don't know yourself unless you know God. If you know God and have a relationship with Him, He will reveal to you who you are. And when you know who you are, you can relate to others. You can't really see the God in others if you don't have a relationship with Him and know who you are.

Let's look at another great scripture in the Old Testament.

*"Thou [God] wilt keep him in perfect peace, whose **mind** is stayed on thee . . ."*
                                                    Isaiah 26:3a

The word for mind here is defined as creative imagination, pattern, image, conception, or mental picture. Whose mental picture is in your mind? At whom are you looking? Where is your imagination? Is it wandering off somewhere on ungodly things, or is it on the Lord? Is God sustaining your imagination? Are you looking at what God's sees for you? God has work for you and me to do, but do we have willing minds? Do we have willing minds to take our candles and go light our world?

What do you think about? As you think in your heart, so you are. I think we have a mega-church, and why shouldn't I?

God created us for increase. We shouldn't want a large church to make us look important. We shouldn't care who gets the credit for it as long as the work of God goes forward, the city is transformed, and people's lives are changed. They're not dying because they have diseases anymore! They're not dying because they're taking too many drugs! They aren't killing themselves because of their bad lifestyles! No. Somebody is making a difference. We have to make a difference. But if we don't get our minds to think the right things, how can we? We have to get out of a pea-brain mentality and begin to think big. Take the city! Take the region! It isn't going to happen unless we get off our rear-ends and start doing something. It is our responsibility to lay hands on the sick and see them recover. It's also our responsibility to reconcile people to Christ, because as Christians we are all to be ministers of reconciliation. (II Corinthians 5:18-19)

You need to think right thoughts – whatever is lovely, true, honest, pure, and of good report. If there is any virtue, if there is anything praiseworthy, think on those things. Think on what you want to happen, not the things you don't want to happen. Don't think about your present circumstances or situation. You may think your church is too poor or too small and that you already have done everything you can do. But none of us have done everything we can do or our churches would be full. There is no small church. God's body is not little. God's church is not small. Anything that God's involved in isn't small. We're working for the Boss – the Big Boss.

Do you want to be in peace? Do you want to be whole, sound, and complete? Let me show you how you can do it.

> *"Thou wilt keep him in **perfect peace**, whose **mind** is stayed on Thee: because he trusteth in Thee."*
>   Isaiah 26:3, emphasis added

The Hebrew word for peace is *shalom*, which means wholeness, completeness, soundness, happiness, health, or well-being. That's what peace is. But the scripture doubles it.

> *"Thou wilt keep him in **perfect peace** whose **mind** is [sustained] by God . . ."*

Perfect means complete, full, something that has come to maturity. The Hebrew word for mind evokes creative imagination, or the picture you see in your mind. God will keep us in "shalom shalom," complete well-being, complete wholeness. I don't know about you, but I want to be whole. I want to be complete. I'm not complete unless I continually renew my mind to think right thoughts.

John told Gaius,

> *"Beloved, I wish above all things that thou mayest prosper and be in health, even as thy **soul** prospereth."*
>   3 John 1:2

You cannot prosper and be in health unless your soul is prospering. Your soul is your understanding, your intellect, knowing how you can receive from God. If you don't understand that the bench is comfortable, you'll sit on the floor. If you don't have an understanding of how to operate something, you'll miss out on it because you don't know how it works. You will back away because of your lack of understanding.

The problem with many of us is that we don't understand what the Word is saying. If we aren't in love with God's Word and don't live our lives by it, we won't be very successful. I know some people may be successful in the natural. They may do some things that work for them, but they are not successful according to God because they're not following His plan. When you follow the plan of God, you will be successful – not just outwardly, where others can see. A man may have a nice suit, a big business, and plenty of money, but is he really prospering – spirit, soul and body? Is he tormented in his mind? Is he happy? God came to make us whole. Jesus came that we might have life and have it more abundantly. "...to the full, till it overflows." (John 10:10 Amp)

You can know the will of the Lord for your life. You can know the mind of Christ because He left us His book. You can know what He's thinking, and what He desires for you, because those things are in His Word.

In I Chronicles 28, David talks to Solomon moments before his death and Solomon's succession to the throne.

9)   *"And thou, Solomon my son, know thou the God of thy father, and serve Him with a perfect heart and with a **willing mind**: for the Lord searcheth all hearts, and understandeth all the **imaginations of the thoughts**: if thou seek Him, He will be found of thee; but if thou forsake Him, He will cast thee off for ever.*

10)   *Take heed now; for the Lord hath chosen thee to build an house for the sanctuary: be strong, and do it."*

I Chronicles 28:9-10, emphasis added

God has chosen us to do something in this generation. We can decide to do it. We can **will** to do it and have a mind to do it, or we can stay in our comfort zones and sit in our houses while the world goes to hell. David told Solomon what God chose him to do. God has chosen us, too, but we have the right to accept or reject His choosing. We can get a mindset of what God has for us, or we can continue on our way and allow the enemy to cheat us out of what God wants us to have.

Many of us are looking at the wrong thing. We have the wrong picture in front of us. We have to get God's picture, God's thoughts, God's ideals, and God's ways in front of us so much that we can't miss them. If I'm not looking at the same picture God's looking at of me, I'm looking at the wrong one. I have to know Him enough that I think His thoughts. I must have my creative imagination sustained by Him because He knows where I'm going better than I do.

God did not make us to be lazy, apathetic, or lethargic, sitting around waiting for someone else to do something. He has a purpose and a plan for our lives, but we have to get His plan and His purpose. We have to get the picture God has for us, and look at it constantly because we can't succeed to anything great in His kingdom without it. We look at great men and women of God — people such as Benny Hinn, Rod Parsley, Marilyn Hickey and Dr. Mike Murdock (a man of wisdom and a great mentor in my life) — and we have to understand that they didn't get there overnight. They didn't get there by watching soap operas or by sitting back, being afraid, and not trusting God. Fear is the opposite of faith, and you can't live that kind of life and be successful in the Kingdom of God.

The Amplified version of I Chronicles 28:9-10 puts it this way: (emphasis added)

9) *". . .Solomon, my son, know the God of your father [have personal knowledge of Him, be acquainted with, and understand Him; appreciate, heed, and cherish Him] and serve Him with a blameless heart and a **willing mind.** For the Lord searches all hearts and **minds** and understands all the wanderings of the **thoughts.** If you seek Him [inquiring for and of Him and requiring Him as your first and vital necessity] you will find Him; but if you forsake Him, He will cast you off forever!*

10) *Take heed now, for the Lord has chosen you to build a house for the sanctuary. Be strong and do it."*

Make up your mind right now to make a difference by doing your part. You must have a willing mind. We need to get a picture of how God wants us here. He wants us perfect, complete, whole, sound, happy, healthy, and in well-being. He wants us to accept what He has for us and be whole. Many people do not have perfect peace. Why? Because they are not looking at a picture of victory. They are not looking at El Shaddai, the God who's all-bountiful, all-sufficient, more than enough, and more than able to sustain them in life. We have to look at our God, who is more than able to help us accomplish what we have to do.

Some say, "Well, I don't need anybody. I can make it on my own, just me and God." Well, let me tell you something. You do need somebody. How do you get to church, work, shopping, etc.? You drive or ride in an automobile that was made by someone. You buy gas that was made, by someone.

You pay a person at a service station that sells the gas to you. You can't do anything in this world without somebody else. No man or woman is an island. You can't make it on your own. You need the help of others.

God wants you to get a picture of what He has for you, and that doesn't mean you can do everything without any assistance. You need the help of other people. And if you don't have that, you're not going to go very far.

It's just like the head, which can only move back and forth, and from side to side. The head tells my hand to reach and my feet to walk and permits all kinds of functions. If I didn't have one of my arms, I could function fairly well but I would be handicapped. I would be missing a very important part of my body. The head can do nothing without the body. It just bobs around. It can't do much. It would be funny . . . the head getting down there and moving something, wouldn't it? If you didn't have two arms, you'd probably have to use your nose or your head to move some things. The head can think. It can tell your body what to do. But, if your body doesn't respond, you're still up a creek. Likewise, the body could not function without the head.

God wants us to see what He sees. God is looking at a picture that He desires. He desires to have unity, because at the place of unity is power and anointing. Psalm 133:2 says the ointment (oil), which is symbolic of the anointing, runs down from the head all the way to the skirt of the garment. So, you see, if the head is anointed . . . if my bishop is anointed . . . that anointing is going to get on me. If your pastor receives anointing . . . if he's blessed . . . it filters down to the body. If I'm honored . . . if my head's honored . . . guess what? . . . my whole body is honored. You have to get a picture of this. Get this thing in your mind. God has some big things for you, but none of it involves defeat and failure. It involves victory. (Jeremiah 29:11) It involves working with other people at a common goal to see something done.

> *"Anything Unrecognized Becomes Uncelebrated.*
> *Anything Uncelebrated Becomes Unrewarded.*
> *Anything Unrewarded Eventually Exits Your Life."*
> *– Mike Murdock*

What you don't recognize, you won't celebrate. Something that is uncelebrated will eventually exit your life. We need to begin to celebrate the life of God in each other and begin to open our eyes and see the life of God that is operating in our brothers and sisters around us, because God has a plan. It doesn't involve us by ourselves.

You see I can't build the church that God wants in my city by myself. I don't have the ability. I don't have the resources. I don't have what it takes, so to speak, in the natural. What will make it happen is not Thomas Meares, but my availability and my willingness to say, "Okay, God, I accept what You are showing me, and what You are saying to me." I'm looking at a picture of victory and not defeat. I'm looking to Jehovah-Nissi my banner of victory. I'm looking to Jehovah-Jireh who sees my need and provides for it. I'm looking to Jehovah-Rapha, who is my healer, and the one who makes bitter experiences sweet. I'm looking at a God who is my Shalom. Hallelujah. He is the peace that passes and transcends all understanding. I'm looking at a God who is more than enough to lead me where He wants me to go. Really, it has little to do with me. I just decided to look at the picture God gave me, and keep looking at it, until it becomes reality.

A group of grandchildren once played a joke on their grandfather. He had one of these big, nice handlebar mustaches. While he was taking a nap, they went into his bedroom and smeared Limburger cheese in his mustache. He woke up and sniffed. "Boy, it stinks in here," he said. He went out of the bedroom into the kitchen and smelled again. "Boy, it stinks in here, too," he said. He went into the dining room and smelled again. "Man, it just smells terrible in this house," he said. Finally, he went outside in the yard, took a big breath, and said, "My goodness, the whole city stinks!"

What you have to do as a child of God is to get rid of the Stinkin' Thinkin' mentality. You have to stop thinking you don't have the talent or resources to do what you need to do. Where God leads you, He will provide.

When Elijah was hungry and thirsty, God sustained him. He went to a brook and ravens brought him bread and meat. You may think your ravens have died, and your brook is dry. You need somebody to nudge you and remind you that God has another place for you. Don't sit there looking at a dry brook and a dead raven. You're looking at the wrong picture — a picture of defeat. God did not create you to stay there. He has a widow woman in Zarephath who's going to sustain you, and she doesn't even know it yet because you haven't yet arrived. When you do, God will bless you both. (I Kings 17:2-16)

Some people walk around sick and unhealthy. One reason is that they are always talking about how they feel and what a doctor said. They're talking about a bad report.

They have a picture of problems, diagnoses, and diseases. That's what they're constantly thinking about and seeing. They walk in sickness, and they are defeated in health because they're not looking at the God who heals — Jehovah-Rapha. Everyday, I say these words, "I walk in healing and health. God, I thank You that You are the God who heals all my diseases. You are my Jehovah-Rapha." If sickness hits me, I don't run to the doctor . . . I run to THE Doctor. I run to Jehovah-Rapha. I put my trust in Him and walk in healing and health.

I'm blessed coming in and going out. I'm blessed in the city and in the field.

3) *"Blessed shalt thou be in the city, and blessed shalt thou be in the field."*

6) *"Blessed shalt thou be when thou comest in, and blessed shalt thou be when thou goest out."*
Deuteronomy 28:3,6

I'm blessed and highly favored of God. I'm one of God's favorite children. Praise God. You are His favorite, too.

Thought. It's what is formed in the mind. If something in your mind is saying that you are schizophrenic, you had better kick it out. If you have a picture in your mind that you're bound, troubled, sick, or poor, and you're just a worm in the dust, you had better get rid of that mentality. God says He takes pleasure in the prosperity of His servants.

". . . Let the Lord be magnified, which hath pleasure in the prosperity of His servant."
Psalms 35:27

Did you know that God wants to bless you so much? When some of you get to heaven, you are going to see all the things that were waiting for you. You didn't have to go lacking for anything. You're going to see those things you could have had, and you're probably going to faint. All you had to do was accept and receive what was already yours.

God wants you to be successful and have a good journey. He wants you to have joy in the journey, but that's something you may have to fight for. If any of you are struggling with that, just live one day at a time for Jesus. Get up, go to a secret place, seek God, read His Word, and put Him first. Say, "Lord, be the Lord of my life today. Help me to be a blessing." Go through that day, let it be a blessed day, and then get up and do the same thing tomorrow. You must make plans to be successful every day by renewing your mind to God's way of doing and being right.

Paul in the book of Romans tells us about the importance of the renewing of our minds.

1) *"I beseech you therefore, brethren, by the mercies of God, that ye present your bodies a living sacrifice, holy, acceptable unto God, which is your reasonable service.*
2) *And be not conformed to this world: but be ye transformed by the **renewing of your mind**, that ye may prove what is that good, and acceptable, and per-fect, will of God."*

Romans 12:1-2

"Be not conformed to this world." What is the scripture saying? It's telling us not to let the world dictate the way we live our lives. We should not be conformed to its customs and fads and the way that we are told to climb the ladder of success by the world.

"*. . . but be ye transformed . . .*" The word 'transformed' means "metamorphosis," the way a caterpillar turns into a butterfly. God wants us to be transformed, changed into beautiful people.

"*. . .by the renewing of your mind . . .*" Although Christ had to go to Calvary and all of hell came against Him, He chose to fulfill the will of the Father, no matter what it took. Be renewed, transformed, by the renewing of your mind.

What are we looking at? What are we thinking about? God doesn't have thoughts for defeat in our lives. He has thoughts to bless us and bring us prosperity. We need the same kind of mentality.

It is estimated that we have as many as two thousand thoughts everyday. What we need to do is grab the good thoughts and do something for God with them. All the bad ones, we need to cast away. When we renew our minds to God's way of thinking, we're not looking at defeat. We're looking at a life of blessings, prosperity, health, and having what we need so we can give to the poor — not just enough to bless us and our families.

Some people say they don't want much, only enough to bless themselves and their families. That's a selfish attitude. There are people dying and going to hell while we live in our comfort zones. Folks, there is a job to be done, and unless we renew our minds to God's ways and what He sees for us, we will never get the job done.

4) *"For the weapons of our warfare are not physical, [weapons of flesh and blood], but they are mighty before God for the overthrow and destruction of strongholds,*

5) *[Inasmuch as we] refute arguments and theories and reasonings and every proud and lofty thing that sets itself up against the [true] knowledge of God; and we lead every **thought** and purpose away captive into the obedience of Christ (the Messiah, the Anointed One)."*

II Corinthians 10:4-5 (Amp)

Verse 5 in the King James Version reads:

*"Casting down imaginations, and every high thing that exalteth itself against the knowledge of God, and bringing into captivity every **thought** to the obedience of Christ."*

When you begin to have thoughts against God's Word, you need to pull them down quickly. You need to say, "No, that is not God's way of thinking. I will not think that way, not for a moment. I am a child of God. I am washed in the blood. I am healed by the stripes of Jesus. I will not receive that thought, that way of thinking or that way of seeing. I see it only the way God sees it."

Why is it important to have God's thoughts? Because you will move toward the things that dominate your thoughts. Why should you not have thoughts of lust and greed and all kinds of bad things? Do you know why serial killers and those that prey on young people and those who perform perverted acts do the things they do? Often, it's because that's what they've been looking at and focusing on for a long time. They watched violence and killing, and they became killers themselves. They watched pornography and looked at all kinds of perverted things, and they became what they saw. They gravitated toward their dominant thoughts.

That's why you have to renew your mind. If you don't do it, you're not going to be successful for God or bless anyone else because you're in bondage to your own self-portrait. You're going to stay in bondage as long as you're looking at the wrong picture.

I can tell what you're thinking about when you open your mouth. I can listen to your conversation and know where your mind is. You had better get prepared. If you get the right picture, you will be prepared. When you look at God's picture, you will begin doing what it takes to see it happen.

Now get rid of small thinking, defeated thinking, bad-job thinking, low-pay thinking and a mentality of living on the backside of the tracks. *You Decide Your Future By The Thoughts You Think.*

You Will Only Possess What You Can Confess

Chapter Three

You Decide Your Future By The Words You Say

20) *"A man's belly shall be satisfied with the fruit of his mouth; and with the increase of his lips shall he be filled.*
21) *Death and life are in the power of the tongue: and they that love it shall eat the fruit thereof."*

Proverbs 18:20,21

By doing a word study, (using the Strong's Bible dictionary) you will find that verse twenty could read like this "A man's emptiness (lack or need) shall be filled to satisfaction with the reward of his **words**; and with the produce of his **speech** (or words) he shall have more than enough." According to this scripture, you can speak increase and blessings into your life. Right words, when spoken, can bring you satisfaction. You are going to eat the fruit of the words you speak, whether you speak life or whether you speak death. You can speak increase or decrease . . . life or death . . . it's up to you. You must understand that every word you speak becomes a living thing to minister or destroy.

20) *"My son, attend to my **words**; incline thine ear unto my sayings.*
21) *Let them not depart from thine eyes; keep them in the midst of thine heart.*
22) *For they are life unto those that find them, and health to all their flesh."*

Proverbs 4:20-22

If God's Word has become real to you, then you have found it and you are speaking it. In the above scripture, you see that speaking God's Word is life and health.

*"Thou art snared with the **words** of thy mouth, thou art taken with the **words** of thy mouth."*

Proverbs 6:2

According to this verse, you can bring destruction upon yourself by the words you speak. Your words can condemn you, or your words can acquit you.

*"For by thy **words** thou shalt be justified, and by thy **words** thou shalt be condemned."*

Matthew 12:37

Doesn't that sound like deciding your future? By your words, you will be justified or condemned. You decide your future by the words that you speak.

Let's look at Mark 5:25-29, emphasis added. This is powerful.

> 25) *"And a certain woman, which had an issue of blood twelve years,*
> 26) *And had suffered many things of many physicians, and had spent all that she had, and was nothing bettered, but rather grew worse,*
> 27) *When she had **heard** of Jesus, [she] came in the press behind and [she] touched His garment."*
> 28) *For she **said,** if I may touch but His clothes, I shall be whole."*

You have to hear something first. Once you hear, you have to do something. The woman heard, and she came. Most importantly . . . she spoke. She said something. There is power in your words.

Now, I want you to notice something. You can speak your healing, or you can speak your wholeness. There's a difference. Think about the ten lepers. Jesus healed all ten of them, but He made one whole. It was the Samaritan. He told the ten lepers to show themselves to the priests, but the Samaritan wasn't a Jew. So he returned to give thanks to Jesus. And Jesus said, "I have made you whole." (See Luke 17) There is a difference in *healing* and *wholeness*. He healed nine of them, but some parts of their bodies may have been missing. The Samaritan was made whole, meaning he was made complete. The word "whole" means complete, sound, or full. I don't know about you, but I want to be made whole. Nothing missing. Nothing broken. Whole. I want Him to speak peace to me because that means wholeness, soundness, and completeness. Let's read verse 28 and verse 29 again.

28) *"For she **said**, If I may touch but His clothes, I shall be whole.*

29) *And straightway the fountain of her blood was dried up; and she felt in her body that she was healed of that plague."*

Notice that the woman with the issue of blood put her miracle in motion by what she **said**. When she heard, she **said**, she came, and she touched. With her mouth, she decided her future. She decided what she was going to have by speaking it. She had spent everything she had, had gone to all the doctors and specialists, but she didn't get any better. She spent all her living. But when she began to take hold of something and **speak** it, her miracle was released.

In this next verse of scripture you will see the power of Gods Words.

*"Through faith we understand that the worlds were framed by the **Word** of God, so that things which are seen were not made of things which do appear."*

Hebrews 11:3

God framed His world by His words. You can do the same because you are made in His image and after His likeness. (Genesis 1:26) Now look at all the verses in Genesis where God framed or created His world by the words He spoke.

3) *"And God **said**, Let there be light: and there was light."*

6) *"And God **said**, Let there be a firmament in the midst of the waters, and let it divide the waters from the waters."*

9) *"And God **said**, Let the waters under the heaven be gathered together unto one place, and let the dry land appear: and it was so."*

11) *"And God **said**, Let the earth bring forth grass, the herb yielding the seed, and the fruit tree yielding fruit after his kind, whose seed is in itself, upon the earth: and it was so."*

14) *"And God **said**, 'Let there be lights in the firmament of the heaven to divide the day from the night; and let them be for signs, and for seasons, and for days, and years."*

20) *"And God **said**, 'Let the waters bring forth abundantly the moving creature that hath life, and fowl that may fly above the earth in the open firmament of heaven."*

24) *"And God **said**, Let the earth bring forth the living creature after his kind, cattle, and creeping thing, and beast of the earth after his kind: and it was so."*

26) *"And God **said**, Let us make man in our image, after our likeness: and let them have dominion over the fish of the sea, and over the fowl of the air, and over the cattle, and over all the earth, and over every creeping thing that creepeth upon the earth."*

Genesis 1: 3,6,9,11,14,20,24, 26

Now that we see how God spoke things into existence, let's see what Jesus said we could do by the power of our words.

> 23) *"For verily I say unto you, That whosoever shall **say** unto this mountain, Be thou removed, and be thou cast into the sea; and shall not doubt in his heart, but shall believe that those things which he **saith** shall come to pass; he shall have whatsoever he **saith**.*
>
> 24) *Therefore I say unto you, 'What things soever ye desire, when ye **pray**, believe that ye receive them, and ye shall have them.'"*

Mark 11:23-24

The action of speech is mentioned three times in verse 23. Notice the words in bold and underline them in your Bible.

In these scriptures, Jesus was talking to His disciples. Are you a disciple and a follower of Jesus? If so, you're included in this invitation. It is true that the seasons in your life will change every time you decide to use your faith. If there is a mountain in your way, and you believe God will move it, He will move it. But you have to **speak** to it. You have to **say** the words.

Let's look at the parable of the prodigal son. Jesus is telling this story.

> 11) *". . . A certain man had two sons:*
>
> 12) *And the younger of them said to his father, Father, give me the portion of goods that falleth to me. And he divided unto them his living.*

13) *And not many days after the younger son gathered all together, and took his journey into a far country, and there wasted his substance with riotous living*

14) *And when he had spent all, there arose a mighty famine in that land; and he began to be in want.*

15) *And he went and joined himself to a citizen of that country; and he sent him into his fields to feed swine.*

16) *And he would fain have filled his belly with the husks that the swine did eat: and no man gave unto him.*

17) *And when he came to himself, he* **said**, *'How many hired servants of my father's have bread enough and to spare, and I perish with hunger!*

18) *I will arise and go to my father, and will* **say** *unto him, Father, I have sinned against heaven, and before thee,*

19) *And am no more worthy to be called thy son: make me as one of thy hired servants."*

Luke 15:11-19

What happened here? No man gave unto him. He decided his future by the seeds he sowed. He sowed to the flesh; he reaped corruption. He was living in a pigpen. He chose his future in the pigpen by the seeds he sowed. But then he also decided his future for the better by what he **said**. He said, "I'll go to my father's house." And what happened?

20) *"And he arose, and came to his father. But when he was yet a great way off, his father saw him, and had compassion, and ran, and fell on his neck, and kissed him.*

21)   *And the son **said** unto him, Father, I have sinned against heaven, and in thy sight, and am no more worthy to be called thy son.*

22)   *But the father said to his servants, 'Bring forth the best robe, and put it on him; and put a ring on his hand, and shoes on his feet:*

23)   *And bring hither the fatted calf, and kill it; and let us eat, and be merry:*

24)   *For this my son was dead, and is alive again; he was lost, and is found.' And they began to be merry."*

Luke 15:20-24, emphasis added

He decided his future by the words he said, but he put some action with the words and reaped a good harvest.

If you're saying the wrong things, you must change your vocabulary. The only way that you are going to succeed is to begin changing what you are saying. If you continue to get the same results with what you are saying, it doesn't take a rocket scientist to figure out that you need to change it. Maybe you've heard the statement "If it's to be, it's up to me." This is true. It's what you say that brings a bright future or a dim future, a blessed future or a cursed future. You can call it like you want it.

Allow me to give you a personal experience. I'll never forget what Bishop Francis Suza (A great Bishop over several hundred churches in Kenya, Africa.) said to me at the close of a men's conference. The Pastor had asked him to pray for all the ministers. When Bishop Suza prayed for me he said, "Man of God you must change your vocabulary." He then paused, and what he said next, though simple was profound to me. "You must speak only Gods

Word," he said. I had thought that I was a man of faith and was doing a pretty good job of aligning my speech with Gods Word. After these words from Bishop Suza I asked the Holy Spirit to help me to only speak what was in line with Gods Word. Since then I have made much progress in this area, however I am still working on speaking only Gods Word.

It is so vital that you understand the power of your **words**. A good friend of mine, the Rev. James Spencer, said the ancient Hebrews understood the importance of their speech because they believed their words became reality. In other words, if one said something, the thing would come to pass. Is that not what happened when the world was created, when God spoke, and His words went forth to create and form what He called for?

The following is an excerpt from Rev. Spencer's teaching on "The Trinity in the Old Testament."

In the Hebrew language, the words for 'word' and 'thing' are the same. To the Hebrews, a word was a thing that was real and dynamic. When a word came out of one's mouth, the Hebrew understood it as something separate from the person who spoke it. The word was a living thing that would become what had been said. This can be illustrated by a comic strip where dialogue appears in balloons above the drawings. Our idea of words is that they go out and somehow get lost, but to an ancient Hebrew the words came out in a balloon and stood there.

If I say, "Bless you," then out of my mouth would come a big balloon with those words in it. It would then leave me and go over to you. The word, once spoken, would become an entity all by itself and do what I had spoken. An entity is a being, an existence, a thing that is independent, separate or self-contained. It has objective or physical reality, but is distinct in its being or character.

When the Word of God became an entity all by itself, it became reality in its own right with its own character and attributes. Now we can begin to understand why the scriptures caution us about watching our words. Psalm 19:14 mandates: "Let the words of my mouth, and the meditation of my heart, be acceptable in thy sight, O Lord, my strength and my redeemer." In ancient Hebrew culture, a word not only revealed something about a person but also went to do what had been revealed. They understood a word as the self of the speaker; but once spoken, that word became distinct and had a personality of its own. When Hebrews spoke about God's Word, they were very careful because they saw the Word as God. The Word of God was God speaking to them. The Word was a distinct, alive, and powerful entity that was coming to them — not only to reveal something, but to accomplish what the Word had spoken. Scriptures such as Isaiah 55:10 and 11 illustrate this point.

"For as the rain cometh down, and the snow from heaven, and returneth not thither, but watereth the earth, and maketh it bring forth and bud, that it may give seed to the sower, and bread to the eater:
"So shall my Word be that goeth forth out of my mouth: it shall not return unto me void, but it shall

accomplish that which I please, and it shall prosper in the thing whereto I sent it."

Do we realize what is hidden here? Do we really see what God is telling us? God says His Word has gone out of His mouth, and He speaks of it as having gone from Him because He said it would return unto Me having accomplished that whereunto I sent it. The Word is God Himself, yet seems to be a distinct person from God who spoke it.

Read Isaiah 31:2:

"Yet He also is wise, and will bring evil, and will not call back His words: but will arise against the house of the evildoers, and against the help of them that work iniquity."

This is the same idea, that God has spoken His Words and they cannot be retracted. Isaac illustrates this truth when he blesses his two sons, Jacob and Esau. Jacob fooled his father and Isaac laid his hands on him and blessed him — the words came out of his mouth. Esau later came in and, realizing what Jacob had done, asked his father to bless him. However, Isaac could not retract the words that had already been spoken over Jacob. Esau could not be blessed because Isaac had already blessed Jacob and could not retract his words or change his mind.

To many of us this is hard to understand because words are often cheap in our culture. So what if I spoke them, I'll just forget them. But Hebrews could not do that because when they spoke a word, that was it —

their words could not be retracted because they had gone on their way to accomplish their purpose. The word was the self of the speaker but once spoken, the word became an entity all by itself and could not return.

If we could get this ingrained in our spirit minds, it would revolutionize our lives and we would watch our words because we cannot take them back. Once spoken, they have gone from us to accomplish what we have said.

Notice the following scripture in Isaiah.

"The Lord sent a word into Jacob and it hath lighted upon Israel."

Isaiah 9:8

The word fell on Jacob like a bomb because once the word was spoken, it was something so real that it could do what had been said. Is that not what happened when the world was created, when God spoke and His words went forth to create and form what He called for?

". . . Even God, who quickeneth the dead, and **calleth** *those things which be not as though they were."*

Romans 4:17b

It is so important that you call for those things that you want, instead of continuing to call it like it is. You can't continue to harp on present circumstances. If you want harmony in your family, begin to call for family harmony. If you want your body to be healthy, begin to call for a healthy body. You have to call for the things you want instead of talking about the way things are. By doing this, you're speaking according to the Word of God. God said He wants you to be healthy. He wants you to have healthy relationships. He wants to bless you and make you prosperous. You can have all those things if you speak the right words — God's Word.

It hasn't been easy to say the right things in every situation. I've been tempted to say it like it is. Well, if that's the way you want it, then say it like that. If not, you should not be saying it like it is. You should be saying it like you want it to be. I'm not denying that the circumstances aren't there, and the situation is not the way it is. I'm not living in denial. I know it's the way it is, but I don't have to allow it to stay like that. I don't have to reinforce it and allow it to stay that way, because I can call it what I want it to be. I can ask God for the change to come, believe Him, and trust in Him, until it comes. And while I'm waiting on it to come — if it still looks like it has gotten worse — I can keep thanking God that the problem is solved and my situation and my circumstances are changing. I'm not giving up. I'm going to say what I want it to be until it becomes what I'm saying it is.

When it is tough, just keep pressing on. Keep saying what you want your life to be like. There will be struggles in your daily life. It's a daily climb. It's a daily routine of pressing on and deciding to pursue God and speaking the right words. You decide your future! You can know where you're going to be because you spoke it, and you're the prophet of your life. You call the shots. God made you that way. He gave you dominion, authority, and the right to use the name of Jesus. Don't sit around in poverty and sickness and just merely get by. God wants you to have a bright, vibrant, vivacious future. ***You Decide Your Future By The Words You Say.***

Notes

Your Obedience To Do God's Word Will Determine Your Success In Life

Chapter Four

You Decide Your Future By What You Do

"I can DO all things through Christ which strengtheneth me."

Philippians 4:13, emphasis added

DO. That's a big little word in this chapter. You decide your future by the things you do. *"I can DO all things through"* whom? Christ. It's not my ability it's my availability. I can't do it by myself. I don't have the smarts, but I can do things through Him because He has already been where I'm going, and He knows exactly what it will take to get me there. The same thing goes for you. Many of you are waiting on God to do something, but notice the Word says, "**I** can **do** all things." We are the doers — not God. Now let's look at some benefits of being a doer of the Word.

*"All the commandments which I command thee this day shall ye **observe to do**, that ye may live and*

multiply, and go in and possess the land which the Lord sware unto your fathers."

Deuteronomy 8:1

There are benefits for **doing** the Word of God. **Observing** and **doing** the commandments in the Word of God will bring you great rewards. One of the benefits is "that you may live..." Now, if you want to die pretty quick, just say and do what comes to you naturally . . . what was taught to you that really doesn't agree with God's Word. You can extend your life by doing what the Word says. The Bible says obey your parents that your days may be long on the earth. There are also things you can do that will cause your life to be shortened. You can drink and carouse and burn the candle at both ends, so to speak, and you will get old quickly. Some people who went to school with me look as if they're about ten or fifteen years older than I am because of the way they've lived. They didn't do the same things I did. I'm pursuing God, and I believe when you're after God, God will preserve you.

What's another benefit when you do God's Word? You're going to multiply. You're going to increase. You're going to go in and possess the land that the Lord promised to give you. God wants to give you your promised land, but you must do the Word of God. You have to be willing to pursue and reach for what God has for you because it's not going to fall out of the tree like ripe cherries. You have to do some pursuing yourself. You can only receive God's blessings by your doing.

Let me give you the definition of the word do. In Strong's Bible Dictionary, it's the Hebrew word *asah*, which means to make, to create. The root word means to work, to labor, toil, make, create, construct, build, to accomplish, to acquire, earn, to procure, prepare, offer, to sacrifice, to appoint, to constitute, to keep and to fulfill. When you *asah*, you become something, and by doing you become. If you don't do, you don't become. The basic meaning of *asah* is do or make, in a general sense. It connotes ethical obligation or obedience. There are always rewards for doing the Word of God. If you are one who **does** His word, you're blessed.

When God says to do something, we need to do it. We need to step out in faith, and do it because faith without works is dead. You don't even have faith if you don't show your works or actions. (James 2:17)

In the account of Christ's birth, the Holy Spirit brooded over Mary, and what was conceived in her was of the Holy Ghost. She had to carry Him. She had to give birth to Him. After she gave birth, she also had to nurture and take care of Him. God may have spoken to you or given you prophecies, but you must nurture them. It's your responsibility to watch over those words from God, and become what God is saying. How do you think the ministers many of you see on TV got where they are? They did the Word, and they kept doing the Word. They nurtured it, watched it, and gave attention to it. They didn't put the words the Lord spoke to them on a shelf. They embraced what He said. People such as Benny Hinn, Joyce Meyers, Rod Parsely, Billy Graham, and Oral Roberts have been successful because they pursued what God has said to them. We need to do the same. We've only been hearing, and we've turned into professional hearers. The Bible says you shall know the truth, and the truth will make you free. (John 8:32) Knowing truth implies that you make it a part of your everyday life.

Let me give you an example. I could say I'm going to come over to your house and take you to a steakhouse, but those would be worthless words if I didn't get in my car, drive over to your house, pick you up, and go to the restaurant. Those are actions. You must have corresponding actions when you read God's Word. When you agree with what God's Word says about your life or a specific revelation you've received, you can't just let it be. You have to nurture and pursue it.

Sometimes God can tell you something, but you have to wait for the right time to act. That timing is the gestation period. God will give you a word or a revelation, but just because He speaks to you, doesn't mean you're an expert yet. When God speaks to us, we tend to get excited. We think, "Wow, God said this!" and we start telling everyone. Sometimes the excitement gives us a sensation of expertise. We think we know everything because God gave us a revelation. If He gives you a revelation, you need to say, "God, what does this revelation mean? What exactly do you mean by this, and how am I supposed to carry it out?" That's the gestation time. That's the time that you carry and nurture what He has given you. You must do your part in giving birth to your word from God.

> *"And it shall come to pass, if thou shalt hearken diligently unto the voice of the Lord thy God, **to observe** and **to do** all his commandments which I command thee this day, that the Lord thy God will set thee on high above all nations of the earth."*
> Deuteronomy 28:1

What's the Lord saying here? If you'll observe to do his commandments, his statutes, his laws, He will set you on high above all the nations of the earth. The word for nations is translated "ethnos" — where we get the words ethnicity and ethnic. See, God is saying if you'll do what I say to do, if you'll obey my Word and my commandments, I will set you up high above all the other ethnic groups of the earth. If you do what God wants you to do, He's going to exalt you above other people. Does that mean you get a big head? No. It just means He has chosen to honor you because you honored Him. The moment you begin to honor Him and His Word, He automatically honors you and lifts you high above your enemies. Then people see the glory of God. The glory of God is on you because you've been lifted up, and they see the reflection of His glory radiating from your life. God's grace, His divine influence on you and your heart, is reflected through your life. How are you going to win people if they don't see his glory?

"And all these blessings shall come on thee, and overtake thee, if thou shalt hearken unto the voice of the Lord thy God."
Deuteronomy 28:2

He's talking about blessings overtaking you. That means they're running you over. This is the blessing of doing the Word. It says, "if thou shalt hearken unto the voice of the Lord thy God." What's the prerequisite of the blessings overtaking you? Listening to the voice of the Lord and obeying Him, which implies doing.

When you're heeding, listening, and doing, the scripture says you shall be blessed in the city and blessed in the field. And you can read all the way through Deuteronomy 28:1-14. It tells about all the blessings that God's going to give you. But this works both ways, as we see in the following verse.

> *"But it shall come to pass, if thou wilt not hearken unto the voice of the Lord thy God, to **observe to do** all His commandments and His statutes which I command thee this day; that all these curses shall come upon thee, and overtake thee."*
>
> Deuteronomy 28:15

When you read the curses, you'll find some bad things there. It is not because God is a bad god. He gave you a choice. You decide your future by what you **do**. You can go out and live like hell, go to nightclubs and slip off and sleep with everybody and his dog, so to speak, drink all the liquor you can drink and burn the candle on both ends. Guess what? You're the one who will look as if you're fifteen or twenty years older than you really are. You're the one who's going to feel bad. You're the one who's going to have all these negative consequences for your actions.

Your choice is your decision. Those two things sound the same, but they aren't. To have a choice you must have different options. Then you can make a choice. But making that choice is your decision.

> 58) *"If thou wilt not **observe to do** all the words of this law that are written in this book, that thou mayest fear this glorious and fearful name, THE LORD THY GOD;*
> 59) *Then the Lord will make thy plagues wonderful and the plagues of thy seed, even great plagues, and of long continuance, and sore sicknesses, and of long continuance.*

60)   *Moreover he will bring upon thee all the diseases of Egypt, which thou was afraid of; and they shall cleve unto thee."*

Deuteronomy 28:58-60

Now King James has a strange way of putting it, saying God is going to make your plagues wonderful. When we think about the word wonderful, we usually think of something good. But this verse uses the word wonderful in a bad sense.

Why would God make your plagues wonderful? Because you didn't follow His instructions. These are God's instructions. If you'll be obedient to His instructions, you'll reap the rewards. If you don't, (as in the Monopoly game), don't expect to pass Go. Don't expect to collect $200. Just expect to go to jail, and stay there in bondage until His Word frees you. The Word will make you free. You shall know the truth, and it will make you free. It's the truth that you're living, acting, and **doing**.

*"Only be thou strong and very courageous, that thou mayest **observe to do** according to all the law, which Moses my servant commanded thee: turn not from it to the right hand or to the left, that thou mayest prosper whithersoever thou goest."*

Joshua 1:7

In other words, you will prosper if you read the Word, follow it and don't try to take away from it or add to it. You just **do** the Word, and you're going to prosper. You can't fail. You're going to get the same results Jesus did. You're going to get the same results the disciples got if you obey the Word.

*"For not the hearers of the law are just before God, but the **doers** of the law shall be justified."*

Romans 2:13

*"For it is not merely hearing the Law [read] that makes one righteous before God, but it is the **doers** of the Law who will be held guiltless and acquitted and justified."*

Romans 2:13 (Amp)

Hearing the Word read is not enough. It has to become *Rhema,* the living word in you.

If you want to be justified, you must be a **doer** of the Word. That's the only way. The definition for the word "do" or "doer" in the New Testament (which would be the Greek) is to make or do, expressing action either completed or continued. You have completed some things, but you're still in the process of working on others. The Bible says those who endure to the end shall be saved. What does it mean to endure? It certainly implies action. You just keep putting one foot ahead of the other. You might not go very fast, but if you're pursuing and pressing toward the mark for the prize of the high calling of God in Christ Jesus, you're going to be blessed. (Phil 3:14 KJV)

22) *"But be ye **doers** of the word, and not hearers only, deceiving your own selves.*

23) *For if any be a hearer of the word, and not a **doer**, he is like unto a man beholding his natural face in a glass.*

24) *For he beholdeth himself, and goeth his way, and straightway forgetteth what manner of man he was."*

James 1:22-24

It would be like me going up to a mirror with saliva running out of my mouth, my hair sticking up all over, smudges on my face, and then forgetting what I looked like. Not **doing** anything about it. I saw myself in the mirror, but I did not correct my appearance. I had faith enough to look, and to hear the Word, but I **did** nothing about it.

You can't afford to look into the Word, find the prescription, go home, and set it on the shelf. God has already given you the roadmap to success. He's already given you the instruction manual. The Bible says in the second book of Peter 1:3 that He's already given us everything that pertains to life and godliness. We have to look into the law of liberty, but we can't just look into it and walk away. We must look into it and do what it says.

*"But whoso looketh into the perfect law of liberty, and continueth therein, he being not a forgetful hearer, but a **doer** of the work, this man shall be blessed in his **deed**."*

James 1:25

What happens sometimes, if you're not careful, is that the devil will come along and steal the Word that was sown into your heart. Why does that happen? Maybe your heart was not prepared, and you couldn't receive the Word. It fell on stony ground or by the wayside, so to speak, and the enemy came along and devoured it. God wants us to be prepared to receive His Word, and if you're prepared to receive it, it's going to go down deep. When God's Word gets deep in your heart, it will cause you to do good works. Now you have become a doer.

I love the way James 1:25 reads in the Amplified version.

*" But he who looks carefully into the faultless law, the law of liberty, and is faithful to it and perseveres in looking into it, being not a heedless listener who forgets, but an **active doer** (who obeys), he shall be blessed in his **doing** (in his life of obedience)."*

What does it mean to look carefully into the faultless law of liberty, to be faithful and persevere in looking? It means you keep doing. You keep looking at God's Word. You can't receive all you need from God in one sitting. You can't go by a drive-thru window and get enough. You need to come in, sit down, and eat awhile. Instead of fast food, you need a seven-course meal. You need something that will last you.

In the last part of verse 25, we see the word obedience. Remember that the word "do" gives a connotation of obedience. You have to follow and complete the instructions in the Word so you can be blessed. God rewards your obedience. He rewards you for following his instructions. What are the rewards of following instructions? The rewards of completion. ***You Can Be Blessed By What You Do.***

13) *"Ye call me Master and Lord: and ye say well; for so I am.*

14) *If I then, your Lord and Master, have washed your feet; ye also ought to wash one another's feet.*

15) *For I have given you an example, that ye should **do** as I have **done** to you.*

16) *Verily, verily, I say unto you, The servant is not greater than his lord; neither he that is sent greater than he that sent him.*

17) *If ye know these things, happy are ye if ye **do** them."*

John 13:13-17, emphasis added

Jesus is talking about servanthood here. If you want to be great in the Kingdom of God, you have to become a servant because everyone serves in heaven. You must learn how to serve others.

One Sunday morning, when I was riding to church, I said, "Lord, my truck sure does need washing. I sure wish You'd let somebody come along and wash my truck for me." Then He asked me whose truck I had washed. That morning in the worship service, He spoke to me again and told me to have the car of a church member washed, and I made it happen the next day.

Again, verse 17 says that if you know and **do** these things, you will be happy. It's your decision to be happy by helping others.

You can't be a concert pianist if you never buy a piano, practice, or take any lessons. If you wanted to be a concert pianist, you would pursue those things. Don't say you want to be a successful business owner if you aren't trying to establish a business. Don't say you want to be a soul-winner — somebody who wins the lost — if you aren't witnessing to anyone. Don't say you want to have nice things if you don't have a job and aren't even looking for one. I could really get into some things here, but I think you get the picture.

You decide your future by what you do, not by what someone else does. The actions you take to improve your life are what decide your future. I can blame something on my wife. I can say she's mean to me and has such a bad attitude and never wants to cook supper for me. I could say that and blame things on her, but my reactions to her create my future. I can create a big, full-blown argument, or I can speak a kind word and turn away wrath and arguing. (Proverbs 15:1)

It has been said that what you do first determines what God does next. You can line up with what God says, and you can receive what He has for you. You can't blame your situation on what has happened. You can't blame the way you are on what happened in your past. You have to go on from here and put your past to rest, forget it, and live with a bright future in mind.

If you want to be successful, you can. It's all about what you **do**, not what someone else does. God has all kinds of blessings in store for you. Everything you will ever need in life, God has. But if you don't decide to reach out and take what God has, you'll never have it. *You Decide Your Future By What You Do.*

Notes

The Highest Pleasure God Will Ever Experience Is When You Exercise Your Faith In Him

Chapter Five

You Decide Your Future By Exercising Your Faith

Using your faith produces your future. What is faith? Faith is belief. Faith is conviction. Faith is trust. Faith is reliance. If I say I have faith in you, it means I have trust in you and I believe in you. In a sense, you can say faith is your conviction — what you believe. The Bible refers to "taking the shield of faith." What does that mean? The Word of God that you believe forms the shield of faith. That's what you use "to quench all the fiery darts of the wicked." (Ephesians 6:16) In other words, you use your shield of faith to block the attacks of the enemy. Your shield of faith is your belief system, which is formed by your understanding of the Word of God.

You will not change your belief system until your belief system is unable to produce something that you need or you desire. That's when we change our belief system — when it won't produce what we're looking for or what we need.

The Bible says in Hebrews 11 . . .

1) *"Now **faith** is the substance of things hoped for, the evidence of things not seen.*
2) *For by it the elders **obtained a good report**.*
3) *Through **faith** we understand that the worlds were framed by the word of God, so that things which are seen were not made of things which do appear."*

Hebrews 11:1-3, emphasis added

The faith these people had produced something. Through their belief, trust, and conviction, they obtained a good report. They decided their future by using their faith.

Actually, fear is faith – in reverse. You can have faith in the negative, or the wrong thing, and you are deciding to have that kind of future. Sometimes we put faith in the wrong things, but the Holy Spirit will correct us if we'll let Him.

Your faith is producing something for you. Someone might say, "Well, when you get over forty, you're going to have to get glasses so you can read." My brother John, who is thirty-five, works with a woman who's just a little older than forty, and he teases her because he can read without glasses. He'll walk two or three feet away from something and read it to her just to show her how well he can read. She says, "It's too small!" and he just walks off. She says, "That's all right. You'll be forty pretty soon!"

But what did the Bible say about Moses? The Bible said that his strength was not abated, which means he was not weak in old age. He was still strong, and his eyes were not dim. In other words, he had 20/20 eyesight.

". . . Moses was an hundred and twenty years old when he died: his eye was not dim, nor his natural force abated."

Deuteronomy 34:7

Many people say it's a fact of life that when you get old, you begin to lose things – your eyesight, your hearing, and your hair. It might be a fact of life, but I want you to notice what Caleb said after he went through the wilderness forty years and finally crossed the Jordan River into Canaan:

10) *"And now, behold the Lord hath kept me alive, as he said, these forty and five years, even since the Lord spake this word unto Moses, while the children of Israel wandered in the wilderness: and now, lo, I am this day fourscore and five years old.*

11) *As yet I am as strong this day as I was in the day that Moses sent me: as my strength was then, even so is my strength now, for war, both to go out, and to come in.*

12) *Now therefore give me this mountain, whereof the Lord spake in that day; for thou heardest in that day how the Anakims were there, and that the cities were great and fenced: if so be the Lord will be with me, then I shall be able to drive them out, as the Lord said.*

13) *And Joshua blessed him, and gave unto Caleb the son of Jephunneh Hebron for an inheritance."*

Joshua 14:10-13

The mountain Caleb asked for had giants in it, but he said, "Give me the mountain. I'm strong. I can possess it." For forty years he had to go with the rest of the crowd and hear them murmur and complain. He had to put up with a crowd of whiners for forty years, but still he kept an excellent spirit and attitude. That's the mark of a true believer — someone who is using his faith. Caleb used his faith and what happened? His request was granted. He was given the mountain. He threw the giants off the mountain and took it. Praise God. It was his inheritance. He decided his future by using his **faith**. **HE** did it! Not his grandmother or grandfather, or his father or mother, or sister or brother. He did it himself. He made the decision.

You and I have to take responsibility for our decisions, and we have to make our faith strong. Our faith and our convictions are made up of many different things. Some of it came from our mothers and fathers and some came from our grandparents. It came from our Sunday school teachers when we were young, our schoolteachers and others who helped shape our beliefs. But, if what we believe is not based on the Word, we need to change it. If we become defensive when somebody begins to talk about something with which we don't agree, we need to examine what we believe, and ask ourselves: Is what I'm thinking, the way I'm believing, and the way I'm living backed up by the Word? Is it what God's saying about the matter, or am I following my own beliefs?

I was saved in a Pentecostal Freewill Baptist Church, and the teachings and beliefs of the people there formed my belief system, in part. Several examples: I was told I should get a job as a plumber instead of being a farmer because I farmed tobacco. Using tobacco was a sin to them, and growing tobacco meant I was wrong. I know that's a little controversial, but being a plumber is a dirtier job than farming tobacco, I think. Also, I was told I should shave my mustache and never let my hair grow past my ears. Those are things that can get inside you and become part of your beliefs and the way you look at things, but are they necessarily true? Are these things right, according to God's Word?

Another thing I was taught was not to buy anything on Sunday. We weren't even supposed to buy a can of soda or go out to eat. Even if a singing group or a preacher came to church with cassettes or books to sell, we didn't buy them on Sunday. Furthermore, they weren't allowed to set up their merchandise in the church. They would have to set it up on the church porch or maybe on their tour buses. Later, my wife and I traveled around singing gospel music, and we sold tapes as a way of supporting our ministry. Some preachers would allow it, but only if we set up our tapes outside the church.

I know there is a balance. You can take things to the extreme and make God's House a house of merchandise. Jesus drove the people out of the temple, and don't you think He was some wimp, either. He drove probably about three hundred people out of there. He turned over the moneychangers' tables and set the doves free. He came through the temple with force. The Spirit of God was on Him. He had some holy anger.

However, I found out that many of the things people believe are based on misunderstandings. They interpreted scripture a certain way, and it became their belief system. It became their faith. If you say or do something they think isn't right, they throw up their shield of faith in defense. Some Christians are wonderful people, but they don't believe in speaking in tongues or the Holy Ghost. They love God but when you begin to talk about the Holy Ghost and speaking in tongues, they throw up their belief systems, saying tongues are of the devil or were only for the early church.

We decide our future by using our faith, or our shield of faith. It's a part of our life. But we must speak God's Word only. When our beliefs are not supported totally by the Word, we need to change them because they aren't going to produce what we really need.

*"By **faith** Abel offered unto God a more excellent sacrifice than Cain, by which he obtained witness that he was righteous . . ."*

Hebrews 11:4a, emphasis added

God accepted Abel's offering because he brought the first fruit in faith. He believed and trusted that when he brought it to God, he was sacrificing it to God. He believed God would accept it, and there would be something waiting on the other side of his offering. He did it in faith. And the scripture said

". . . God testifying of his gifts: and by it he being dead yet speaketh."

Hebrews 11:4

Now look at Hebrews 11:5

*"By **faith** Enoch was translated that he should not see death; and was not found, because God had translated him: for before his translation he had this testimony, that he pleased God."*

Enoch went to heaven without dying physically. He was taken up to heaven because he took God at His Word and lived his life accordingly, which pleased God. The reward for an obedient, faith-filled life — a life that follows the Word — is heaven. Your reward is being in the presence of God forever.

How do we please God? What is the ultimate pleasing of God? When we walk by faith. When we believe Him. When we use our faith to receive what God says is ours. It pleases God when He tells you to do something and you, in faith, obey.

"If ye be willing and obedient, ye shall eat the good of the land:"
Isaiah 1:19

What does your obedience say? It says you trust the person who asked something of you. If my little girl gets up on top of a wall, I tell her to jump down and let me catch her. If she has trust and faith in me, she will be obedient and jump right into my arms. If we really trust God and have faith in Him, we will be obedient. When we're obedient, we prove that we believe Him.

I know this is simple. If I have faith in someone, it means I believe that person and what that person says. If that person promises to give me something and all I have to do is meet them somewhere to receive it, I'm going to do it. And because of my faith in that person, I will receive what I believed the person would give me. It's the same way with God. If God speaks to you and you believe Him, you will be obedient. On the other side of your obedience is the reward that God said He was going to give you. We decide our future when we use our faith.

Some people say they have no faith. They do, but their faith is working in reverse. It's taking them down the wrong route. They have faith that their hair is going to turn gray. They have faith that their teeth are going to fall out or their eyes are going to get dim. They have faith that they're going to get cataracts. People joke about these things, but we need to use our faith to get what we desire, not what we don't. I don't want to have gray hair. I don't want my teeth to fall out so I can't chew my food or my eyes to go dim so I can't see.

"The Highest Pleasure God Will Ever Experience Is When You Exercise Your Faith In Him."

The highest pleasure that God will ever have is when you believe Him. When you say, "I know my Father will do what He says He'll do!" When we do this, God says, "Look at my children down there, talking and acting just like Me. They know they have a good God." He gets excited! It pleases Him. On the other hand, it pains Him most of all to be doubted. Our unbelief hurts Him more than anything.

> *"But without **faith** it is impossible to please him: for he that cometh to God must believe that he is, and that he is a rewarder of them that diligently seek him."*

Hebrews 11:6

Those who seek God diligently will be rewarded. How much is diligent? A little bit more. Somebody said a fanatic is somebody who loves God a little bit more than the next person. If that is the case, let me be a double fanatic. He rewards those who **diligently** seek Him, those who use their faith over and over and over, and keep moving toward what God's Word says. They keep saying, "Lord, this is what Your Word says." They keep praying the Word, speaking it, living it, walking in it, and because of that, they are rewarded.

If we could see things the way God does, two or three weeks probably would be like fifteen or twenty seconds. It's like my little girl coming to me and asking me what time it is. About five minutes later, she'll ask me the same question because she's anticipating something, and she keeps on asking. Many times, we're that way with God. When are you going to do this, Daddy? You said You were going to do it. When are you going to do it, God? We just need to say thank You, Father. I know You're going to do it because You said You're going to do it. I give You praise. I give You glory. Whenever You're ready, Lord, I'm ready.

> 7) *"By faith Noah, being warned of God of things not seen as yet, moved with fear, prepared an ark to the saving of his house; by the which he condemned the world, and became heir of the righteousness which is by faith.*
> 8) *By faith Abraham, when he was called to go out into a place which he should after receive for an inheritance, obeyed; and he went out, not knowing whither he went."*
>
> Hebrews 11:7-8

Notice that it was by faith that Noah became an heir of righteousness. It was also by faith and obedience that Abraham went toward the Promised Land.

> *"By faith the walls of Jericho fell down, after they were compassed about seven days."*
>
> Hebrews 11:30

After Joshua had done, by faith, what the Lord told him to do, the walls fell down. God told Joshua to walk around the walls once daily for six days and then seven times on the seventh day. On that day, the Lord had told him, he would shout and the walls would fall down. Because Joshua had faith in God, the walls of Jericho fell, even though they were so thick that chariots could run along them. Nothing else could knock down those walls. They didn't have cannon balls or gunpowder at that time. It was impossible. But because they used their faith and believed God was a true and honest God, the walls came down. Joshua told the people to be quiet as they walked each day. They were walking out in the hot sun, marching around the walls of the city, and the people of Jericho were probably yelling and heckling them. Imagine how hard it might have been to stay silent. It took faith. They had to trust in Joshua and believe in God. When they did, the walls fell down. On the seventh day and the seventh time around, all they had to do was shout! Praise God, the walls fell down. They went in and destroyed a strong, fortified city that couldn't have been taken by anyone else. Because of their faith, it happened. They conquered an unconquerable city.

> *"By faith the harlot Rahab perished not with them that believed not, when she had received the spies with peace."*
>
> Hebrews 11:31

The rest of the city did not believe. They laughed at this Jehovah God. They laughed at the children of Israel as if they were the giant talking to David. But Rahab, a harlot, believed them. She took them in, hid them, and let them out another way so they wouldn't be killed. And the scripture says she didn't die with those who didn't believe because she had "received the spies with peace." She befriended them. She decided her future. She could have slammed the door in their faces and refused to help them because they were foreigners. Something must have caused her to have faith in them because the Word tells us she didn't perish with the unbelievers. It implies that she believed God sent them and because she did, her life was spared. She decided her future by using her faith.

> 24) *"By faith Moses, when he was come to years, refused to be called the son of Pharaoh's daughter;*
> 25) *Choosing rather to suffer affliction with the people of God, than to enjoy the pleasures of sin for a season;*
> 26) *Esteeming the reproach of Christ greater riches than the treasures in Egypt: for he had respect unto the recompense of the reward."*
> Hebrews 11:24-26

Moses could have lived like a king his entire life. However, he refused the treasures of Egypt and became the deliverer God called him to be. It was only by faith that he fulfilled his destiny.

In the following scripture, notice what happened to Moses in the tabernacle, because he chose to believe God.

> 8) *"And it came to pass, when Moses went out unto the tabernacle, that all the people rose up, and stood every man at his tent door, and looked after Moses, until he was gone into the tabernacle.*

9) *"And it came to pass, as Moses entered into the tabernacle, the cloudy pillar descended, and stood at the door of the tabernacle, and* **the Lord talked with Moses**.

10) *And all the people saw the cloudy pillar stand at the tabernacle door: and all the people rose up and worshipped, every man in his tent door.*

11) *And* **the Lord spake unto Moses face to face, as a man speaketh unto his friend**. *And he turned again into the camp: but his servant Joshua, the son of Nun, a young man, departed not out of the tabernacle."*

Exodus 33:8-11, emphasis added

Like Moses, I would rather forsake all the riches and treasures of Egypt to be able to speak face-to-face with my God. I know that if I have that kind of relationship with Him, I will not lack for anything. Friends share secrets. Moses spoke to God face-to-face. You can also be a friend of God by deciding to use your faith. *You Decide Your Future By Exercising Your Faith.*

Notes

The Place Of Agreement Is A Place Of Accomplishment

Chapter Six

You Decide Your Future By Finding The Place Of Agreement

18) *"Verily I say unto you, Whatsoever ye shall bind on earth shall be bound in heaven: and whatsoever ye shall loose on earth shall be loosed in heaven.*

19) *Again I say unto you, That if two of you shall **agree** on earth as touching any thing that they shall ask, it shall be done for them of My Father which is in heaven.*

20) *For where two or three are gathered together in My name, there am I in the midst of them."*

Matthew 18:18-20

Jesus is talking about the place of agreement, which is a place of power. Agreement is the essence of the Godhead.

"And God said, Let Us make man in our image, after our likeness . . ."

Genesis 1:26a

The scripture uses the pronoun "us" to describe God, meaning that the Father, Son and Holy Ghost agreed.

The word for "God" throughout the first chapter of Genesis is the Hebrew word *Elohim*, which is the plural name for "God" – God the Father, the Son, and the Holy Ghost. They were in agreement in the beginning to create Heaven and Earth, and later in verse 26 to create man. Praise God for agreement!

You decide your future by your ability to agree. Look at the scripture Matthew 18:19 again. It says that if two or more of us agree, the Father will do anything we ask.

Offense will kill a heart of worship in people. When you are offended, you can't really worship. How can two walk together unless they agree? (Amos 3:3) If you're out of agreement with your brother, you can't really come into the presence of God in worship. If you love God and live in His presence, you won't be offended by your brother or sister. You just can't do it.

22) *"But I say unto you, That whosoever is angry with his brother without a cause shall be in danger of the judgment: and whosoever shall say to his brother, Raca, shall be in danger of the council: but whosoever shall say, Thou fool, shall be in danger of hell fire.*
23) *Therefore if thou bring thy gift to the altar, and there rememberest that thy brother hath ought against thee;*

24) *Leave there thy gift before the altar, and go thy way; first be reconciled to thy brother, and then come and offer thy gift.*

25) ***Agree*** *with thine adversary quickly, whiles thou art in the way with him; lest at any time the adversary deliver thee to the judge, and the judge deliver thee to the officer, and thou be cast into prison."*

Matthew 5:22-25, emphasis added

I can't love God without loving you. If I get offended with you, I'm still obligated to love you.

20) *"If anyone says, I love God, and hates, (detests, abominates) his brother in Christ, he is a liar; for he who does not love his brother, whom he has seen, cannot love God, Whom he has not seen.*

21) *And this command (charge, order, injunction) we have from Him; that he who loves God shall love his brother (fellow believer) also."*

1 John 4:20-21(AMP)

The heart of God is for us to be one. As Jesus was one with the Father, He wants us to be **one**. That's a place of power. That's a place of agreement.

On the day of Pentecost, the one hundred twenty followers of Jesus were there in one accord. They were of one mind. They were waiting on the promise of Jesus and all of them had come to a place of agreement. What happened on the day of Pentecost? The Holy Spirit came, baptized them, and endued them with power. (Luke 24:49)

"But ye shall receive power, after that the Holy Ghost is come upon you: and ye shall be witnesses unto Me both in Jerusalem, and in all Judaea, and in Samaria, and unto the uttermost part of the earth."

Acts 1:8

*1)   "And when the day of Pentecost was fully come, they were **all with one accord** in one place.*

2)   And suddenly there came a sound from heaven as of a rushing mighty wind, and it filled all the house where they were sitting.

3) And there appeared unto them cloven tongues like as of fire, and it sat upon each of them.

4) And they were all filled with the Holy Ghost, and began to speak with other tongues, as the Spirit gave them utterance."

Acts 2:1-4

Your strength comes from the Holy Ghost, who empowers, enables and anoints. Being in one accord is what I feel allowed the Holy Spirit to come and endue them with power. Now, let me give you an example of the power of agreement. If a waiter at a restaurant doesn't treat you exactly right, you can be disagreeable and you'll get a certain level of service in return. If you can find an agreeable factor with the waiter, however, you can turn things around and get a better level of service. There is power at the place of agreement.

Let me give you a power key, as Pastor Thomas Michael calls it. In his book, "The Agreement Unlocking the Favor of God," he says:

> ### *"The Fruit of Agreement Is Favor."*
> ### *– Pastor Thomas Michael*

The Father and Son were in agreement, and agreement = power. What happened when Jesus said what the Father said? Blind eyes opened. Deaf ears heard. Lepers were restored. Religious demons were stirred up. (John 10:24-39)

The children of Israel murmured and complained, grumbled, and griped. What happened to them? They wandered around in the wilderness until all those in doubt and unbelief died. In essence, they said, "Would that we were back in Egypt. We had cabbage, broccoli, squash, potatoes, black-eyed peas, and cornbread. We had plenty." (See Exodus 16:13) They didn't believe that God, who was leading them out, could sustain them and take care of them. They were disagreeable with Him, and it brought them death.

> ### *"The Place Of Agreement Is*
> ### *A Place Of Accomplishment."*

You have to find the agreeable factor in every situation. On what can we agree? That's the place of power. The place of agreement is a place of accomplishment.

The greatest agreement you will walk in is with your spouse.

> *"Therefore shall a man leave his father and his mother, and shall cleave unto his wife: and they shall be **one flesh**."*
>
> Genesis 2:24

The traditional Christian marriage vows describe a covenant made between a man and a woman. The scripture says a man "shall leave his father and mother and be joined to his wife and the two shall become **one flesh."** (Genesis 2:24) You see, there's power when two become one. My wife and I are in agreement, and that is a strong and wonderful place.

*". . . If two of you shall **agree** on earth as touching any thing that they shall ask, it shall be done for them of My Father which is in heaven."*

Matthew 18:19

The church is probably operating at about a ten-percent margin of agreement. Can you imagine what would happen if all the people who came to church were of one mind and accord? Can you imagine the impact that would have on this world?

Instead, you have one sister sitting in one place, and another sister sitting across the church, and they've had an argument. They are offended with one another and aren't agreeing on anything. That affects the body of Christ and keeps them and us from encountering the presence of God.

Sometimes, when you are pressing in during praise and worship and you're getting right to the throne, about to enter into the Holy of Holies, it seems like it's just hard to get there. You may wonder why this happens. If everybody would get in agreement and begin to worship God, we could access His presence. We have to be in one mind and one accord, as they were on the day of Pentecost. They were there for a common purpose, and it wasn't *my* ministry, *your* ministry, *my* church, or *your* church. They were together in one mind and one accord, waiting on Jesus' promise that He would ask the Father to send another comforter, the Holy Ghost. We must find that place of agreement, as well, because that's where we find power.

Watch the heart of God in this next scripture. Jesus is speaking.

9) *"I pray for them: I pray not for the world, but for them which Thou hast given me; for they are Thine.*

10) *And all mine are Thine, and Thine are mine; and I am glorified in them.*

11) *And now I am no more in the world, but these are in the world, and I come to Thee. Holy Father, keep through Thine own name those whom Thou hast given Me, that **they may be one**, as We are."*

John 17:9-11, emphasis added

Note that last sentence. That they may be one, "as We are." He knew that at the place of oneness and the place of unity was POWER!

Why do you think the devil fights the leadership of the church, keeping them from coming together and finding what they can agree upon? They may not agree on every point of doctrine, but they can agree on the absolutes of scripture — that Jesus is the Christ, and that He came to redeem us to the Father. The heart of God has always been to have one family, not a divided family. He wants unity, because it allows us to stand. Recall this statement from our pledge of allegiance: "One nation under God, indivisible, with liberty and justice for all." There is a place of agreement, and it produces results.

Now, let's move on to verse 20 in John 17. Here, Jesus is praying for the church. He says:

"Neither pray I for these alone, but for them also which shall believe on Me through their word . . ."

Whose word is He talking about? The disciples' word. The words the disciples spoke — which were passed on to them by Jesus and given to Him by God are still being spread today in our attempt to follow the disciples' lead.

*"That they **all** may be **one**; as Thou, Father, art in Me, and I in Thee, that they also may be **one** in Us: that the world may believe that Thou hast sent Me."*
                                    John 17:21, emphasis added

How is the world going to believe in God? I feel it will be when they see the oneness and unity of the church. When the church becomes unified, there is power and the dead are raised, the blind see, deaf ears are opened, and crippled legs walk. Miracles are performed, and the world cannot deny them because they see the product of unity. They see power manifested.

I don't know if this is doing anything for you, but I'm telling you that the place of agreement, unity, and oneness is the heart of God.

You can't have the gold without the glory. Don't think you're going to have blessings unless you're in God's presence. Everything you have and everything that comes to you will come to you from being before Him and in His presence. You must have His presence because when you walk in His presence, you will be more agreeable. You will look for the agreeable factor in every situation.

Now, let's go to Matthew 19:16-22.

16) *"And, behold, one came and said unto Him, Good Master, what good thing shall I do, that I may have eternal life?*

17) *And He said unto him, Why callest thou Me good? There is none good but one, that is, God: but if thou wilt enter into life, keep the commandments.*

18) *He saith unto him, Which? Jesus said, Thou shalt do no murder, Thou shalt not commit adultery, Thou shalt not steal, Thou shalt not bear false witness,*

19) *Honour thy father and thy mother: and, Thou shalt love thy neighbour as thyself.*

20) *The young man saith unto Him, All these things have I kept from my youth up: what lack I yet?*

21) *Jesus said unto him, If thou wilt be perfect, go and sell that thou hast, and give to the poor, and thou shalt have treasure in heaven: and come and follow Me.*

22) *But when the young man heard that saying, he went away sorrowful: for he had great possessions."*

The young man was offended in what Jesus asked him to do. And what did that cause him to do? He went away sorrowful. He's the one that lost because he allowed himself to be offended in what Jesus asked him to do. You don't find any agreement here.

Recall that in Matthew 11:2-5, John the Baptist was in prison. Before they beheaded him, he sent his disciples once again to Jesus. They asked Him, *"Art thou He that should come, or do we look for another?"* Jesus sent them back to tell John the Baptist about the miracles and all the things they had seen – restored sight to the blind and restored hearing to the deaf. Jesus said, *"And blessed is he, whosoever shall not be offended in Me."* (Matthew 11:6) When you're offended in someone, that person cannot bless you. Notice what it said. It said blessed is he who is not offended in Me.

In other words, if you are offended, the opposite happens. Blessings are blocked. If I am offended in someone, it cuts off every blessing from me that could come from that person because I took offense. Now, I can't receive anything from the person who offended me, because I'm not in agreement with them.

Even when you offend people, you still have to recognize God in them and love them. The Bible says to go and be reconciled to them. (Matthew 5:22-25) And, you are the one who should go to them and be reconciled, even if you're not the one who was offended or perceived an offense. If you know someone has been offended, you should seek reconciliation. If you do your part, and still the relationship can't be restored, you are free from it. You have done what you were supposed to do.

One offense or one perceived offense can cancel out all the "atta boys." It's amazing how we can just throw relationships away because of perceived offenses. They block all that God would do through those relationships. They cancel out the place of power and agreement . . . the place where God could do great things with us.

You have to find the place of agreement. You may not agree with everything your brother or sister does, but don't focus on that. You must find agreeable factors with them, and that allows you to find a place of accomplishment. You don't put them down because you don't agree with things they're doing. It's not what they do that should determine what you do. It's how you react to what they do. You have a will and a right to act the way God would act. You don't have to react in the wrong way. Don't blame things on others, when they're nobody's fault but yours. You decide your future when you find the place of agreement.

> *"... if two of you shall **agree** on earth as touching any thing that they shall ask, it shall be done for them of My Father which is in heaven."*
>
> Matthew 18:19

God works in multiples of three. If you and I are in agreement, He's the third one. Jesus said:

> *"For where two or three are gathered together in My name, there am I in the midst of them."*
>
> Matthew 18:20

Jesus is saying that where two agree, **He** is the third factor. **He** is the power factor. **He** is the one who manifests what is being agreed upon. **He** is the one who makes it complete – Hallelujah!!!

> 54)   *"And when He was come into His own country, He taught them in their synagogue, insomuch that they were astonished, and said, Whence hath this man this wisdom, and these mighty works?*
>
> 55)   *Is not this the carpenter's son? is not His mother called Mary? and His brethren, James, and Joses, and Simon, and Judas?*

56)   *And His sisters, are they not all with us?*
Whence then hath this man all these things?
57)   *And they were* **offended** *in Him.   But Jesus*
said unto them, A prophet is not without honour, save
in his own country, and in his own house.
58)   *And He did not many mighty works there*
because of their unbelief."

Matthew 13:54-58, emphasis added

**"The Purpose For Staying Free From Offence Is
To Access The Presence Of God."**

They were offended at Him, and could not believe that He could do these things. They could not recognize Him, and they lost out. They allowed themselves to be offended, because they believed He was Mary's son, someone too familiar to do anything of great importance.

Because they were offended, they were not blessed. He could not do many mighty works because of their unbelief and offense toward Him. When people offend you, you're judging them and that affects your ability to receive from them.

I refuse to be offended by you because I need you. I need what God has deposited in you. I must reach out, receive, and embrace what you have. God has given you those things so you can be a blessing to me and help me do what I have to do.

The purpose for staying free from offense is to access the presence of God. Let's look at Matthew chapter 15.

1)   *"Then came to Jesus scribes and Pharisees,*
which were of Jerusalem, saying,

2) *Why do Thy disciples transgress the tradition of the elders? for they wash not their hands when they eat bread.*

3) *But He answered and said unto them, Why do ye also transgress the commandment of God by your **tradition**?*

4) *For God commanded, saying, Honour thy father and mother: and, He that curseth father or mother, let him die the death.*

5) *But ye say, Whosoever shall say to his father or his mother, It is a gift, by whatsoever thou mightest be profited by Me;*

6) *And honour not his father or his mother, he shall be free. Thus have ye made the commandment of God of none effect by your tradition.*

7) *Ye <u>hypocrites</u>, well did Esaias prophesy of you, saying,"*

8) *This people draweth nigh unto Me **with their mouth**, and honoureth Me with their lips; but their **heart is far from Me**.*

9) *But in vain they do worship Me, teaching for doctrines the commandments of men.*

10) *And He called the multitude, and said unto them, Hear, and understand:*

11) *Not that which goeth into the mouth defileth a man; but that which cometh out of the mouth, this defileth a man.*

12) *Then came His disciples, and said unto Him, Knowest thou that the Pharisees were **offended**, after they heard this saying?*

13) *But He answered and said, Every plant, which My heavenly Father hath not planted, shall be rooted up."*

Matthew 15:1-13, emphasis added

Notice that the scribes and Pharisees, who were religious leaders, could never find a place of agreement with Jesus. Therefore, they never could receive what only He was capable of giving them. They were offended because Jesus told the truth about them. (verse 12)

The following statements are power keys on agreement.

- *The **Fruit** of Agreement Is **Favor.***

- *The **Attitude** of Agreement Is **Submission.***

- *The **Force** of Agreement Is **Obedience**.*

- *The **Character** of Agreement Is **Humility**.*

- ***Offense** Is the Enemy of **Agreement**.*

– Pastor Thomas Michael

Let me leave you with one last agreement key.

"Everything that exists came into being through the power of agreement, from the Godhead on down."

When you enter into agreement with someone and something good comes of it, it comes through the power of agreement. ***You Decide Your Future By Finding The Place Of Agreement.***

Notes

Your Seed Of Time Will Determine The Quality Of Your Relationships

Chapter Seven

You Decide Your Future By Your Relationships

You decide your future by your relationships, and the most important relationship you will ever have is with the Holy Spirit. It is out of this relationship with the Holy Spirit that everything else will come. The Bible says in Matthew 6:33 that if you seek first the Kingdom of God and His righteousness – God's way of doing things and being right – then all these things will be added unto you.

> *"But seek ye first the kingdom of God, and His righteousness; and all these things shall be added unto you."*
>
> Matthew 6:33 (KJV)

Jesus asked the Father to send the precious Holy Spirit as a Comforter.

"And I will pray the Father, and He shall give you another Comforter, that He may abide with you for ever . . ."

John 14:16

You are deciding your future by the relationships you have. What are the important relationships in your life? It has been said that people are like elevators– they'll take you up or they'll take you down. I have heard Dr. Mike Murdock say that when God wants to bless you, He puts a person in your life. Likewise, he says that when the devil wants to destroy you, he puts a person in your life. We must discern which relationships in our lives are right.

The Bible says we must love everybody, but some people must be loved at a distance. You can't have close relationships with some people because they're not going in the same direction you are. They're not doing the same things you're doing. They don't have the same desires and motives. If you're in a relationship with someone who is going in the opposite direction, you may be influenced to pursue goals or dreams that are not yours. I have heard people say they plan to marry someone as a way of leading that person to Jesus. But the Bible says:

"Be ye not unequally yoked together with unbelievers: for what fellowship hath righteousness with unrighteousness? and what communion hath light with darkness?"

2 Corinthians 6:14

I have a problem with a Christian who says his best friend is a sinner. That person doesn't have his relationship with the Holy Spirit right yet, or his best friend wouldn't be a sinner. I'm not speaking against sinners. God loves them. He hates sin, but He loves sinners. We're supposed to love everybody, but we shouldn't love what they do. We don't love their lifestyles. We want to see them have a relationship with God. When they know the Lord and their relationship is right with the Holy Spirit, we can be in a relationship with them. In the same way, until you have your relationship right with God, it is very hard to have relationships with others.

Jesus was the ultimate sacrifice. All we have to do to have a relationship with Him is accept the sacrifice He made, and the blood He shed for us. We have been redeemed by the sacrifice Jesus made of Himself for us. It's a complete and finished work, and we don't have to work on that. We don't have to work out our redemption because it has already been done. We have to work out our salvation, but we don't have to work out our redemption. Hallelujah. There's a difference.

"Wherefore, my beloved, as ye have always obeyed, not as in My presence only, but now much more in My absence, work out your own salvation with fear and trembling."

Philippians 2:12

Salvation is something we work out as we work on our relationship with the Holy Spirit. Out of that relationship comes a working out of our salvation, health, security, deliverance, and blessing. Praise God. Salvation is not just a fire escape. Salvation causes us to be complete, whole, and delivered, so that we can be a blessing to someone else.

Out of our relationship with the Holy Spirit will come a life that is blessed, a life that is happy, and a life that is joyous because He said that in His presence is fullness of joy. If in His presence there is fullness of joy, where do we need to be? We need to live in His presence. We need to have a relationship with Him like no one else. Out of that relationship we can rightfully relate to others. We're not trying to find joy from someone else because we know we can find it in His presence.

There's a difference between happiness and joy. If people have the power to make you happy, they also have the power to make you sad. But no one can take your joy because in His presence is fullness of joy. The joy comes from a relationship with the Holy Spirit, which no one can take away.

> *"Thou wilt shew me the path of life: **in thy presence is fulness of joy**; at thy right hand there are pleasures for evermore."*
>
> Psalm 16:11

In the original Greek of John 14:16, the word for comforter is *"paraclete,"* which actually means "one who walks along beside you." The Holy Spirit is there beside you, and you can turn to Him anytime, like a helper or one who walks arm in arm with you. That's why He said that at His right hand are pleasures evermore. He is at your right hand, and in His presence is fullness of joy. He lives inside you, but He also walks beside you.

In the Amplified, John 14:16 reads:

> *". . . I will ask the Father and He will give you another **Comforter**, (Counselor, Helper, Intercessor,*

Advocate, a Strengthener, and Standby) that He may remain with you forever."

He comes to live with you when you accept Christ. He comes to live in your heart because the Father sent him when Jesus requested. When Jesus left the earth, He said, "Lord, don't leave them without a Comforter. I've been with them, and I've kept them, Lord, but I want You to send them another comforter." So He sent His very Spirit – the precious Holy Spirit. He is everything you need, and the Holy Spirit was given to you for the purpose of helping you to live an abundant life.

"Even the Spirit of truth; whom the world cannot receive, because it seeth Him not, neither knoweth Him: but ye know Him; for He dwelleth with you, and shall be in you."
John 14:17

Notice, He said, "He dwelleth **with** you, and shall be **in** you." I don't understand all of that, but I don't really understand how air can be all around me and in my lungs, too, and that doesn't keep me from breathing. Even though I don't understand it, I am happy to have Him living in me and walking beside me.

When you're in a relationship with Him and when you're in His presence, nothing else matters. When you're in His presence, the city could burn down around you, and it wouldn't matter. Even though things can go wrong and will, you'll still be a winner because as you walk in His presence, He'll tell you what's happening.

It's so important that we develop our relationship with the Holy Spirit because as we develop it and get in His presence, wrong is exposed. In His presence, everything that's wrong in your life will be exposed. Every bit of darkness begins to come to the light. That's why we need Him. We need to pass everything through the relationship (the sifter of the Holy Spirit) and ask Him, "Holy Spirit, is this right? Is this what You want?"

Let me give you an example. I was praying one morning, and I said, "Holy Spirit, you can't be a leader unless you can be a follower first. That is correct, isn't it?" And He said, "Yes, it is." You've got to be able to follow before you can lead. We have to be willing to submit to one another, to yield to one another in love.

A relationship with the Holy Spirit produces a wonderful life. Out of that relationship comes peace and joy. Peace that surpasses all understanding comes from being in His presence.

There's more about the Comforter in John 14:26.

*"But the **Comforter**, which is the **Holy Ghost**, whom the Father will send in My name, **He shall teach you all things**, and bring all things to your remembrance, whatsoever I have said unto you."*

This is powerful. Jesus is saying that the Father will send the Holy Spirit, the *Paraclete*, the Helper, the Counselor, the Advocate, the Intercessor, and the Standby to represent Him and to act on His behalf and teach you all things. What is the benefit of having a relationship with the Holy Spirit? He will teach us all things.

We decide our future by the relationships we have. And our relationship with the Holy Spirit results in His teaching and showing us all things. But it doesn't stop there. When He teaches you and shows you all things, can you imagine the confidence you'll have? You've met people who think they know everything, and you have seen their confidence. They think they know it all. Everything you've ever seen, they've done. They know all about it. In other words, they're as good as the manufacturer. The manufacturer is the only one who knows everything about the product because the manufacturer is the one who put it together and made it, and the Holy Spirit is the Manufacturer.

He moved upon the face of the waters, (Genesis 1:26) and He was there when God said, *". . .Let us make man . . ."* The word "God" in Genesis 1 is *Elohim,* a plural word that shows the multifaceted nature of God as the Father, Son and Holy Spirit. He knows our frame. He knows all about us. Praise God. He knows we are spirit, soul, and body. We were made in his image and after his likeness. Therefore, we can receive the words of Jesus as the Holy Spirit teaches us and brings them to our remembrance.

We must have the Word. The Word became flesh and dwelled among us, and His name is Jesus. When you have the Word, you have Jesus. And the Holy Spirit is the Comforter and Teacher who makes Jesus so real to you. He will teach you all things and bring to your remembrance what Jesus said. When you read the Word, which is Jesus, the Word begins to become a part of you. When you hide His Law in your heart, that you might not sin against Him, the Holy Spirit is the One who brings to your remembrance the things Jesus said. He can't bring it to your remembrance unless you're in love with the Word, and it's inside you.

We need to have a definite plan to read God's Word because if we don't have His Word in us, the Holy Spirit won't have anything to bring to our remembrance. The Holy Spirit is there to help us.

If you're in a relationship with someone, you share things. If I'm not really close to you, you're not going to share intimate things with me. I'm close to my wife, and our intimacy allows us to share things with each other that we wouldn't share with anybody else. Intimacy is not a bad word. Webster's Dictionary defines it as "marked by very close association, contact, or familiarity." It means being so close to someone that you're able to share secrets.

I love it when the Holy Spirit shares secrets with me. I love hearing the voice of the One God sent to walk beside me, the One Jesus prayed the Father would send so I wouldn't be an orphan, the One sent to Earth to represent the Godhead.

We can tap into the power of the Godhead when we get in agreement with the Holy Spirit. When He speaks to us, and we hear and obey Him, then what He tells us will come to pass. When I say "hear," I mean do something about what He says. If you don't act, you really didn't hear what he said.

*"But when the **Comforter** is come, whom I will send unto you from the Father, even the Spirit of truth, which proceedeth from the Father, He shall testify of Me."*

John 15:26

He is the Spirit of Truth. If He tells you anything, you can take it to the bank. Now, look at John chapter 16:7.

7) *"Nevertheless I tell you the truth; It is expedient for you that I go away: for if I go not away: the **Comforter** will not come unto you; but if I depart, I will send Him unto you.*

8) *And when He is come, He will **reprove** the world of sin, and of righteousness, and of judgment:"*

What did He say He would do when He comes, and you enter into a relationship with Him? He will discern. He will reprove. He said He would reprove, or convict, the world of sin, righteousness and judgment. If you are in a right relationship with the Holy Spirit, your presence will bring conviction on the hearts and lives of people. And the stronger that relationship is when you enter their presence, the more uncomfortable they'll become. If they don't know Jesus, they'll either yield, and come to know Him, or they will exit your presence.

I'll give you an example. It seems like there are different times in your life when you are closer to the Holy Spirit. Recall the familiar story of the footprints in the sand. There were two sets of footprints and then, suddenly, there was just one set of footprints. I think there are times in our lives when we have that kind of experience with the Holy Spirit — we're in His arms, and He carries us. Remember when Moses came down from the mountain after he was given the Ten Commandments? He had to put a veil over his face to cover the brightness that had come from his nearness to the presence of the Almighty.

There was a time after the Lord called me to preach that He pulled me up to Himself and carried me. And when people saw me, they noticed a difference. They saw something changing my life. They saw something on me.

One gentleman walked into my business during this time, and he couldn't even come close to me. He had to take his coat off because he had become hot. He didn't even come over to shake my hand. I don't believe, at that time, this person was in a good relationship with God, and it was the presence of the Holy Spirit on my life that began to convict him of sin.

Remember what the children of Israel said in Exodus 20:19?

". . . Moses, Speak thou with us, and we will hear: but let not God speak with us, lest we die."

In His presence, everything that is not right will be exposed. Sin will be exposed. Wrong thinking and wrong motives will be exposed. In His presence, we become transparent and any darkness shows. In one of his presentations, my good friend Rev. Warren Hunter put up a transparency with the outline of a man on it. Then, he threw a little piece of a napkin that caused a dark spot to appear on the man. I thought that was really interesting because when sin comes in, it brings a part of darkness in you. However, when we get in His presence and walk close with Him, we can be totally transparent. What happens when you're transparent? The glory of God can shine through you, and you can be like Moses when he came down from the mountain. Your skin can shine with the very presence and glory of God, and radiate His power. Others can see the glory on you because all of the darkness is gone. You're transparent. So He's just beaming through you. That's a result of a relationship with the Holy Spirit.

I want to encourage you today to ask God to birth a passion in you for His presence. Ask Him to help you develop a daily habit of entering His presence . . . a daily habit of going into a secret place. Remember the Pharisee who stood on the corner praying his big prayer so men could see him. He had his reward. Everybody who saw him thought he was a godly man; but Jesus told us to go and pray in secret, and God will reward us openly.

I want to encourage you to sanctify a room in your house as a place to meet with the Holy Spirit. Set a time every day to go there and meet Him. Don't make it hard for yourself. Start by promising God ten minutes of each day, and then gradually increase the time you spend with Him.

You may wonder whether the place you choose matters very much. Yes, it does. God created places before He created people. Your place of prayer needs to be one that is sanctified and hallowed, a place where you and He can meet together – not a place where people are running through and phones are ringing.

By setting aside time in a quiet place, you're saying, "Holy Spirit, this is our place and our time." He will share things with you in private that He won't share with you in a public setting. You're the one in control of how He's going to talk to you, and what you and He can have together. It's beautiful. Have a place and a time, and develop that relationship. There is so much that can come out of it. He'll tell you what to do. He'll show you what's coming. He'll warn you about things that are going to happen.

"Howbeit when He, the Spirit of truth, is come,
He will guide you into all truth: for He shall not speak

of Himself; but whatsoever He shall hear, that shall He speak: and He will shew you things to come.

John 16:13

The Holy Spirit is going to speak what He hears the Father saying about you.

Here is the same scripture from the Amplified version:

"But when He, the Spirit of Truth (the truth-giving Spirit) comes, He will guide you into all the truth (the whole, full truth). For He will not speak His own message (on His own authority); but He will tell whatever He hears (from the Father; He will give the message that has been given to Him), and He will announce and declare to you the things that are to come (that will happen in the future)."

You see, you decide your future by your relationship with the Holy Spirit. It is awesome when He tells you things. I love it when He talks to me, when He tells me things to do, when He shows me something to keep me from falling, when He exposes wrong people in my life, when He shows me people that are just there for the bread and the fishes and not for my wisdom.

People will take what God has provided for you if you'll give it to them. But many times they don't want your wisdom. They don't want to know how you earned what you have. They just want what you have. They're not willing to sacrifice. They're not willing to spend time in the secret place. They're not willing to develop a relationship with the precious Holy Spirit, who can tell them everything. The Holy Spirit knows all things. He will tell you what is in the future, if you have a relationship with Him. And that doesn't come from just one meeting.

When I met my wife, I didn't ask her to marry me immediately. We dated and spent time together, and I fell in love with her. I wanted to see her at lunchtime and have lunch with her. At night after work, I'd get washed up and scoot over there right away to spend time with her and have supper with her. After I took her home at night, I wanted to call her again. That's the kind of thing I'm talking about. When we have that kind of relationship with the Holy Spirit, we won't have a problem. Our love will work. We will relate well with other people. We will be able to love them. We will be able to see the things that God wants us to see because the Holy Spirit will expose wrong. He will expose enemies. He will expose that which is not good for our lives. He will show us things that are wrong with our relationships and friends. That will enable you to pray for them. He doesn't show you things so you can go blow your friends out. He shows you things so you can try to help people overcome obstacles. We're made to be a blessing. God made us for His pleasure, and He's pleased when we're giving, when we're instruments He can flow through, touch through, and love through.

I don't want to do anything to hurt the Holy Spirit. I don't want to do anything to grieve Him, but sometimes I do. I did it the other day when I spoke negatively of someone, even though I had only met the person briefly in a phone call. After I'd done it, I felt a heaviness — like something wasn't right. The Holy Spirit told me, "You talked about that person to someone else and made her look bad. You had no right to do that." The next day, I made several calls. It took several tries to reach her, but when I did I apologized to her. At the end of the call, she told me I had made her day. I was willing to say I was wrong, and I also said to the Holy Spirit, "I've already apologized to the person I said it to, but I ask you to forgive me also."

You see, the Holy Spirit will expose your wrongdoings. And when you feel that He's grieved and that something has happened, you need to say, "Holy Spirit, what happened? What did I do?" And He will tell you. Then you can repent and feel Him close again.

Now that I've talked about a relationship with the Holy Spirit, let's talk about relationships with others. You will never get where you're going without being connected and related to other people. We need each other, but first we need to work on our relationship with the One who walks besides us, the One who loves us, and the One who will never leave nor forsake us. He might withdraw sometimes when we do something foolish because we have grieved or hurt him, but He never really leaves us.

One of the determining factors of whether or not a relationship is good for you is how you feel after a person leaves. When you are in the company of someone, and you feel drained after they leave, it may be a sign that the relationship is not a good one. That person is pulling you down and sapping your energy. People come into your life for different reasons. There are people who will come for the loaves of bread and the fish. The prodigal son had friends as long as he had money; but, when he lost it all, he wound up in a pigpen. These people associated with him only when he had something to give them. When he really needed them, they all forsook him. We have to guard our focus. The Bible even says,

"Now I beseech you, brethen, mark them which cause divisions and offences contrary to the doctrine which ye have learned; and avoid them."

Romans 16:17

You don't stop loving or caring about those mentioned in the above verse. However, if they are causing strife and division in your life, you don't need that. We must remove the clutter of unhealthy relationships from our lives.

If you have the right kinds of relationships, you can go to the right place. Even though Joseph was a good man and had an uncommon dream, he still needed good relationships. Some say it wasn't good that he was thrown in a pit and sold to the Ishmaelites, who sold him to the Egyptians, to Potiphar, the captain of the guard to Pharaoh. But God gave him his dream, and God knew the relationships Joseph needed. God knew the circumstances required to bring him to his destiny. Joseph didn't just moan and groan, "Oh, God, I remember what you said about me, but I guess it was a lie, or I guess I misunderstood what You said." Joseph took the circumstances and made the best of them. Wherever he was, he did his best. He had a spirit of excellence.

Joseph went through some hard times and had some bad relationships. His brothers did not like him because of his dreams, and sold him as a slave. Later in Potiphar's house, Potiphar's wife tried to seduce him. He refused her advances, and she lied about him, but he didn't give up. He wound up in prison and made some good relationships there — with a butler and a chef — and finally his relationship with the butler got him out of prison and into the palace.

Relationships can take you down or they can take you up. That's why you need to discern which relationships are good for you, and which ones are bad for you. You need to exit the bad ones gently and kindly, because you never know when someone you are working with may be promoted and become your boss. So even though you can't have relationships with certain people, it doesn't mean you have to treat them like an enemy.

Some may say they want to remain close to their families. We all want that, but what really makes us family? Jesus said,

48) *". . .Who is My mother? and who are My brethren?*

49) *And He stretched forth His hand toward His disciples, and said, Behold My mother and My brethren!*

50) *For whosoever shall do the will of my Father which is in heaven, the same is my brother, and sister and mother."*

Matthew 12:48-50

You may not be able to have a close relationship with your blood relatives. You have to make that choice. Sometimes you have to love them at a distance because they don't understand your dreams or where you're going, and they don't know what God's doing in your life. You need the kind of relationships in which people discern what God is doing with you — the kind of relationships that can help and enhance you on your journey.

If you hang around with a bunch of turkeys, you will never soar like eagles. Your friends influence you. The relationships you permit in your life shape you. When I was in construction work, I hung around guys who wanted to flirt with girls all the time and I noticed that same spirit wanted to jump off on me. That's why I say people are like elevators; some in your life will take you up and some will take you down. You have to discern which ones are not beneficial to your assignment, your dream.

It's not that you don't love those people — you would do anything you could to help them. But not everybody can learn from you. Don't feel bad. Not everybody can learn from me. Some may think I'm too young or too inexperienced. That's okay. I'm not offended. I hope they can find somebody who can teach them something. I'm not sent to everybody, but I'm sent to somebody. I realize my limitations, and I'm not offended.

It is important that you enter into relationships that cause you to go toward your goals and dreams — relationships that won't slow you down. You need to get rid of anything that slows you down. I don't care if it's old office equipment or a bad relationship. You need relationships that speed up your progress with God. Surround yourself with relationships that will help you move more quickly toward your destination.

You need to identify the people who help you get where you need to go. If you are rightly related to someone, don't let the devil or some flashy person come along and make you think you aren't. You need to ask God for discernment and to keep you from walking away from a relationship you need.

Let's look at a few scriptures concerning relationships.

*"Thou shalt not avenge, nor bear any grudge
against the children of thy people, but thou shalt love
thy **neighbor** as thyself: I am the Lord."*

Leviticus 19:18

The word "neighbor" means associate, brother,
companion, fellow, friend, husband, lover. All of these
describe this word. *"You shall love your **neighbor** as
yourself"* refers to someone with whom you share a close
relation. It could be a brother or sister in the faith, those
who are going in the same direction. You are to love and to
relate to those who are your neighbors, your associates. This
does not mean you exclude other people, but work at those
relationships that will lead you into what God has for you.
You are to love all people, but you shouldn't feel obligated
to associate with them if they're not companions, brothers,
fellows or friends.

Turn to Romans 12. This is how we should treat people
with whom we have relationships:

10) *"Be kindly affectioned one to another with
brotherly love; in honour preferring one another;*
11) *Not slothful in business; fervent in spirit;
serving the Lord;*
12) *Rejoicing in hope; patient in tribulation;
continuing instant in prayer;*
13) *Distributing to the necessity of saints; given
to hospitality.*
14) *Bless them which persecute you: bless, and
curse not.*
15) *Rejoice with them that do rejoice, and weep
with them that weep.*

16) *Be of the same mind one toward another.
Mind not high things, but condescend to men of low
estate. Be not wise in your own conceits.”*
Romans 12:10-16

Let me tell you what a man-pleaser is. A man-pleaser is
one who flatters those above him. A man-pleaser seeks to
be nice, good, kind, and sweet and do everything right to
please those above him. However, those who are below him,
he treats like dogs. God says for us not to be high-minded
or snobbish. In our relationships, he tells us to:

*"Live in harmony with one another; do not be
haughty (snobbish, high-minded, exclusive), but
readily adjust yourself to (people, things), and give
yourself to humble tasks. Never overestimate yourself
or be wise in your own conceits.”*
Romans 12:16 (Amp)

In these next scriptures, Paul tells us the only thing we
owe others is to love them. Therefore, when we love them,
we have fulfilled the law of God.

8) *"Keep out of debt and owe no man anything,
except to love one another; for he who loves his
neighbor (who practices loving others) has fulfilled
the Law (relating to one's fellowmen), meeting all its
requirements.”*

10) *"Love does no wrong to one's neighbor (it
never hurts anybody). Therefore, love meets all the
requirements and is the fulfilling of the Law.”*

Romans 13:8,10 (Amp)

Love really is the adhesive that holds relationships together. How can you be rightly related to people if you don't love them? How can you love God, whom you haven't seen, if you can't love those whom you do see? (I John 4:20) How can we who are created from the dust of the earth — whether black, red, yellow or white — be proud of who we are? You can't be proud that you're black or white, or whatever color you are, because we all come from dirt. Some are just a little lighter dirt and others are a little darker dirt.

> ### *"Love Is the Adhesive That Holds Relationships Together."*

We have to love one another, and how can we be in right relationship unless we do? God is love. This is about relationships in a broader sense versus those relationships that take you where you need to be. In relation to loving people in general, I can't throw someone away just because the relationship isn't taking me into my dreams and goals. I still have to give my love and prayers. I have to know that God has a way of connecting them with people they need . . . people who are able to help them discover their assignment and purpose.

Many will be jealous when you announce your goals and dreams because they haven't yet discovered theirs. You know where you are going, and what God has called you to do. But, they don't, and they're going to disagree with you and possibly stand in the way of your goals. However, you have to love those who "despitefully use you and do good to them that hate you." (Matthew 5) Jesus said,

43) *"Ye have heard that it hath been said, Thou shalt love thy neighbour, and hate thine enemy.*

44) *But I say unto you, Love your enemies, bless them that curse you, do good to them that hate you, and pray for them which despitefully use you, and persecute you;*

45) *That ye may be the children of your Father which is in heaven: for He maketh His sun to rise on the evil and on the good, and sendeth rain on the just and on the unjust.*

46) *For if ye love them which love you, what reward have ye? do not even the publicans the same?*

47) *And if ye salute your brethren only, what do ye more than others? do not even the publicans so?*

48) *Be ye therefore perfect, even as your Father which is in heaven is perfect."*

Matthew 5:43-48

Now, look at the 48th verse in the Amplified version:

"You, therefore, must be perfect (growing into complete maturity of godliness in mind and character, having reached the proper height of virtue and integrity), as your Heavenly Father is perfect."

We have to love people even when they are not beneficial to us and couldn't care less about what we do, and where we're going. We still have to love them and ask God to work in their lives. Don't be upset that people are not overjoyed about your dreams. Just discern the value of the relationship and let it be what it is. Have *friendship* with people you can have friendship with, but have *relationship* with those who understand your dreams.

There is a difference in a friend and a mentor. Friends are happy with you just as you are. They don't want to change you. Mentors want to take you to a higher level. They will tell you things you need to know to improve. They will risk upsetting or offending you to get you where you need to go. They will risk your friendship to help you mature and grow.

You need mentors, and you need friends. You need both of these relationships in your life. You need mentors who will lift you to a higher level and give you the information you need to get where you're going. And you need friends with whom you can just relax, with whom you don't have to perform. You can go fishing, bowling, skating or hunting with them and just have a good time.

"Knowing that for whatever good anyone does, he will receive his reward from the Lord, whether he is slave or free."

Ephesians 6:8 (Amp)

> **"What You Make Happen For Others, God Will Make Happen For You"**
> **- Mike Murdock**

If you are doing your best to help someone reach a goal and accomplish a dream, God is going to make the same happen for you. When you take care of HIS House, He'll take care of YOUR house. What we make happen for others — what we help others attain and what we help others do — God will in turn help us achieve our dreams, goals, and assignments. He will bring new people and opportunities into our lives. He will cause someone to give us favor.

"Do nothing from factional motives (through conscientiousness, strife, selfishness or for unworthy ends) or prompted by conceit and empty arrogance. Instead, in the true spirit of humility (lowliness of mind), let each regard the others as better than and superior to himself, (thinking more highly of one another than you do of yourselves)."

Philippians 2:3 (Amp)

Have you ever looked at someone and thought, "Well, I know more than they do," or "I'm closer to God than they are?" I've caught myself doing that very thing. When we do that, we need to recognize it and admit our error to the Lord. In Philippians 2:3, Paul tells the Philippians to think more highly of others than themselves. We should look for the good in others. Even when we see flaws or wrongdoing, we shouldn't let that cause us to throw the baby out with the bath water, so to speak. Many of us are ready to divorce one another just because we get offended or see something wrong. God says not to do that.

"Let each of you esteem and look upon and be concerned for not (merely) his own interests, but also each for the interests of others."

Philippians 2:4 (Amp)

I shouldn't be concerned only about my vision, and what I'm doing. I'm supposed to reach out and help you and see your gifts and callings unlocked. I'm supposed to be concerned not merely about my own interests, but about yours and the welfare of those who are in relationship with me. I can't be selfish and introspective. I have to reach out and help others. Even though they may be on another spiritual level, I have to help them and uplift them.

13) *"For you, brethren, were (indeed) called to freedom; only (do not let your) freedom be an incentive to your flesh and an opportunity or excuse (for selfishness), but through love you should serve one another.*

14) *For the whole Law (concerning human **relationships**) is complied with in the one precept, You shall love your neighbor as (you do) yourself."*
Galatians 5:13-14 (Amp)

Notice that the law concerning *relationships* is to love your neighbor as yourself. This verse ends with loving your neighbor, which is where we started out in Leviticus 19:18. Paul is saying the same thing to the Galatians.

I am going to close this chapter with one last scripture, which comes from the lips of the master.

"Therefore all things whatsoever ye would that men should do to you, do ye even so to them: for this is the law and the prophets."
Matthew 7:12

If you want people to get involved in your dreams and goals, then you must get involved in what God's doing in their lives. If you are not selfish, and you reach out to help others come into what the Lord wants for them, God will help you get where you want to be. That's God's law. It's the way He operates. When you forget about yourself and try to help someone else get somewhere, God's going to see to it that you have the resources and people you need in your life. ***You Decide Your Future By Your Relationships.***

Notes

The Quality Of Your Seed Will Determine The Quality Of Your Harvest

Chapter Eight

You Decide Your Future By The Seeds You Sow

*"Be not deceived; God is not mocked: for whatsoever a man **soweth**, that shall he also **reap**."*
Galatians 6:7

The Amplified version says:

"... that and that only is what he will reap."

Whatever you decide to sow is what you will reap. Many people want to interpret this scripture in a negative sense, saying others are bad and inevitably will reap bad things. It is true that if you sow bad seeds, you will reap a bad harvest. If you sow wild oats, you will reap wild oats. That's why I'm glad that when I was in high school, I never really ran with the guys who did bad things. I have done bad things in my life, but at least I didn't do them in high school.

You decide your future by the seeds you sow, whether they are good seeds or bad seeds. In Matthew 12:33, Jesus talked about making a tree good or bad. You decide the quality of life you want to live by the kind of seed you choose to sow.

My marriage hasn't always been perfect. But it's getting really close to it now and it takes work. If I want my wife to respond favorably to me, I must sow seeds of kindness, care, gentleness, romance, and love . . . maybe even some flowers occasionally. Anything worth having is worth working for. My dad taught me that you have to fight for what you believe. You have to fight for what you want. As Christians, we are kings and priests, (Revelation 5:10) but we have to fight for our future. We have to work for what we desire.

Many people think that when they get to a certain point in their lives, they will be happy. But, no one ever really gets to that point. When you get there, you will be looking for more success. Success is a journey, not a destination.

You can be successful, but you never really arrive at success. It's a journey because when you get to one level of success, you're going to reach for a higher level. God made you and me to reach. You should always be reaching for more. You have to decide. It's your own choice. Man is made up of spirit, soul, and body. The will is part of the soul and is the right to choose. You have a right to will. You have a right to choose. You have a right to decide your future by the seeds you sow.

If you sow seeds of hate, you will reap hate in your future. If you sow seeds of unforgiveness, you will find unforgiveness in your future. If you sow seeds of strife, you will live in strife. If you sow seeds of doubt and unbelief, your future will be filled with doubt and unbelief. If you sow a financial seed into good soil, your future will bring a harvest of financial blessings. You can't buy blessings, but you can sow a financial seed for a particular season of your life — your future.

You are not buying your future with the seed you plant. You are planting a seed against needs that will arise in your future. Look at the scripture again.

*"Be not deceived; God is not mocked: for whatsoever a man **soweth**, that shall he also **reap**."*
Galatians 6:7

When you plant your garden, you don't just throw out any kind of seed. If you want tomatoes, you have to plant tomato seeds. If you want watermelons, you have to plant watermelon seeds. You plant the kind of seed that produces the harvest you want. It is the same way in the realm of the Spirit and in the things of God. You have to plant the right kind of seed. If you plant love, you will reap love. God planted His only Son because He wanted a family. And we are all here, part of the family of God, because of what Jesus did on the cross. The devil tried his best to keep Jesus from being planted as a seed and tried to destroy the seed many times, but he – thank God — was not successful.

One definition of a seed is anything you have that, when sowed, will produce something you didn't have before. There are times when you may think you don't have any seed, but there will never be a time in your life when you don't have any seed to sow. For example, love is a seed. Kindness is a seed. Your smile is a seed, words are seeds, time is a seed, and your gifts and talents can be sown as

131

seed. Money is a seed. I could go on and on, but I think you get the point. There will never be a time when you don't have a seed to sow. You just need to inventory your seeds. God says he will give seed to a sower.

*"Now he that ministereth **seed to the sower** both minister bread for your food, and multiply **your seed sown**, and increase the fruits of your righteousness."*
II Corinthians 9:10

I want to give you two examples of God giving seed to a sower. On the first occasion, I was preaching one Sunday morning and I sensed the Lord telling me to buy a young man some soundtracks. The young man was a very talented singer but didn't have any recorded accompaniment. As I was preaching, I said to this brother, "The Lord said for me to buy you as many soundtracks as you can list for me." Later, I thought, "Wow, how will I pay for all those tracks?" About two weeks later, a sister in my church came to me after a service and gave me $100. When I receive money unexpectedly, I usually ask God what it is for. After asking, He told me it was for the soundtracks He asked me to give the young man.

The second occasion was similar to the first. Again I was preaching, and I felt God tell me to buy a suit for a brother. So, I told him we would go to the men's store and buy one. A few days after that, I had him fitted for a suit. The gentlemen at the men's store dressed him up nicely, and the suit was charged to my account. About a week or so went by, and I was asked to preach for a pastor friend of mine. Afterward he gave me a check for $225. That night, as I was getting ready for bed, I asked God what the money was for and He told me it was for the suit.

Praise God, folks. God's Word works. When He says He gives seed to the sower, you can believe it. If you are obedient to sow, as I was in these two examples, I believe you can expect to receive a harvest in that area of your life. In other words, because of my obedience to sow my seed, I believe that God will provide what I need.

The seeds you sow decide your future. If you have bad eating habits, you will reap poor health. The Old Testament describes different kinds of foods you should eat. (Leviticus 11) The book advises against eating animals with divided hooves, and many of us just love ham, sausage, and pork chops. Dr. Mike Murdock, my good friend and mentor, once said that it takes the body fourteen days to digest a pork chop. Then he added, "You weren't made to tote around a little pig." You know what I did after hearing that? I quit eating pork. I'm deciding my future by what I eat. Have you ever heard the saying, "You are what you eat?" If you sow into good eating habits, you will reap good health. If you exercise — which some of us need to do, including me — your body will feel better. It will function better. Along with eating properly, you will reap good health and the energy and strength to do what you're supposed to do. You decide to have a healthy future by choosing to eat and exercise properly.

People living on the streets, sleeping in abandoned warehouses and houses, are deciding their future. I feel sorry for them, but if they would come and sit down in a life-giving church and listen for about three or four months, they could get off the streets. They have the same opportunity for blessing as anyone else. The cure for poverty and pain is knowing how to get out of it. That's really the only cure – knowing and embracing knowledge, and finding out how to move from a place of poverty to the place of blessing.

Think of the prodigal son. He had squandered all of his inheritance and was living in a pigpen. He wanted to go back to his father's house, but he had sown the wrong seed. He had spent all of his money on friends and what the Bible calls "riotous living." He sowed bad seed, and he reaped a bad harvest. He lost everything he had because he was selfish and wasteful.

> 14) *"And when he had spent all, there arose a mighty famine in that land; and he began to be in want.*
> 15) *And he went and joined himself to a citizen of that country; and he sent him into his fields to feed swine.*
> 16) *And he would fain have filled his belly with the husks that the swine did eat: and no man gave unto him."*
>
> Luke 15:14-16

What happened here? No man gave unto him. Because he sinned and was wasteful, he ended up reaping what that kind of living brings you.

Most of the people living on the street undoubtedly have squandered their earnings. They throw away the money they make on crack or alcohol or other bad habits. Many times ignorance is to blame. Most of us have an ignorance problem, but the real problem is that we don't want to admit it. The Bible says,

> *"My people are destroyed for lack of knowledge: because thou has rejected knowledge, I will also reject*

thee, that thou shalt be no priest to me: seeing thou hast forgotten the law of thy God, I will also forget thy children."

Hosea 4:6

If something is destroyed, it cannot be fixed. The verse goes on to say that if you reject knowledge, you will be rejected. You see, we decide our future! Everyone can be successful by applying the principles of God's Word to their lives.

I am most happy to help people in need; but, if I help, and they refuse godly counsel, I won't continue. They have the same right to decide their future that I do.

Kenneth Copeland preached a series called "You are the prophet of your own life." He said that we are in control because we have a will, and God will not override it. You can say, "I'm not going to church. I'm going to stay home tonight"... and guess what? God isn't going to be in control — you are. You are the one staying home. God wanted to send something to you, but you decided that you were going to pamper yourself and miss what was in your future. You satisfied your present and sabotaged your future. Many churchgoers have done this for years. They want all the comforts. They want a user-friendly church. "Just pat me on the back, make me feel good, tell me everything's going to be all right," they say. "But don't teach me how to get out of trouble. Don't really get into the Word of God and tell me how I'm living and what I have to do to move from where I'm at to a better future." Do you want to be blessed? Be a blessing to someone else. Do you want favor? Decree favor. You first must sow what you want to reap.

On my way to a conference in Texas, my flight was delayed. On that particular airline, there are no assigned seats, so passengers have to go to the counter to get seat assignments and boarding passes. When I got to Atlanta to make my connecting flight to Texas, they weren't giving boarding passes for that flight yet. So, I sat down and started reading the Bible. After half an hour, I went back to the counter and the attendant told me there were no more seats available on the flight. When I told him I had to get on the flight, he sent me to customer service. I went to that counter and began to pray while I was standing in line. I said, "Lord, I need favor. I've got to get on this plane." Just as I was thanking God for favor, the customer service attendant told me she would move me to first class. It was the first time I had ever flown first class, and my seat was upgraded again on my flight home.

Here's what got me. A man came up to the counter while the attendant was helping me and tried to ask her a question. She said something about his flight being canceled, and he got upset. He insulted her and her co-workers, and then threatened to never fly with the airline again. I thought to myself that he was at a place of disagreement, whereas I had tried to be agreeable. By being patient and agreeable, I was upgraded to first class without even asking. I was asking God for favor and being nice, and I reaped the reward. I thanked the woman two or three times. Always thank people when they do something good for you.

Let's look at this scripture one more time.

*"Be not deceived; God is not mocked: for whatsoever a man **soweth**, that shall he also **reap**."*
Galatians 6:7

The Amplified version:

> *". . . that and that only is what he will reap."*

You're going to reap only what you sow. You can't plant corn and expect beans. You can't sow hate and expect love in return. You can't sow deceit and expect people to be truthful to you.

> 8) *"For he that **soweth to his flesh** shall of the flesh **reap corruption**; but he that **soweth to the Spirit** shall of the Spirit **reap life everlasting**.*
> 9) *And let us not be weary in well doing: for in **due season** we shall reap, **if we faint not**."*
>
> Galatians 6:8-9, emphasis added

I mentioned before that people who abuse alcohol, crack, and other drugs sow seeds of a bad habit. They sow it into their flesh, and of the flesh they reap corruption. They may have to sleep in an abandoned warehouse and wake up afraid every ten minutes while their health deteriorates because they're sowing bad seeds.

The problem with many of us is that we get weary in well doing. It may seem like it isn't working, but no matter how long the time is from planting to harvest, you cannot give up. You cannot speak negatively or say it isn't working, because you're negating the whole process. You don't want your harvest to come up mangled, twisted, and weak. You want a bumper crop – a big harvest. And in order to get that big harvest, you must understand and apply the following scriptures.

6) *"But this I say, He which* **soweth sparingly shall reap also sparingly; and he which soweth bountifully shall reap also bountifully.**

7) *Every man according as he purposeth in his heart, so let him give; not grudgingly, or of necessity: for God loveth a cheerful giver.*

8) *And God is able to make all grace abound toward you; that ye, always having all sufficiency in all things, may abound to every good work."*

II Corinthians 9:6-8

God always rewards us for our obedience. Notice that after we obey verse seven, we are then entitled to the rewards of verse eight. We must never give up doing what is right, and that is sowing good seed. Now let's look at Galatians 6:9 again.

"And let us not be weary in well doing: for in **due season** *we shall reap,* **if we faint not.***"*

In the margin of my Bible, it reads "if we do not lose heart." If you don't lose heart, you will reap in due season. I don't know about you, but it is my due season. I have to give you one more powerful testimony. A couple of years ago, I was in a church conference in Winston-Salem, North Carolina, where a prophet friend of mine was preaching. After preaching, he began to call people out and prophesy to them personally. As he was giving a word of prophecy to one young lady, he said, "You love to write. You are a writer." She agreed, and then he asked her if she had a computer and she said, "no." To this he replied, "God is going to give you a computer – and not a junky one, but a nice one with a printer." After that, I didn't hear what else he said to her because God began to speak to me. What He said was surprising. He said, "You're the one who's going to give the young lady the computer." I replied, "God, I don't have any money to buy a computer. You don't mean me, God. There must be someone else here who has extra money or a computer to give away." There were other things I said to myself. I wondered if I should have gone to Winston-Salem another day. After I finished arguing with God I said, "Okay, God, You said you would give seed to a sower, and I'm a sower." At that time, I knew it would take at least $1,000 to purchase a good computer and printer. In order to get the money I decided to sow a seed of $10 and ask God for a hundred-fold return. (see Matthew 13:23 and Mark 4:8)

Three weeks from the time I sowed the $10, a lady came into my office and said she had made a vow to the Lord and hadn't kept it. Because of her disobedience, she felt she was experiencing family problems. After we talked a few minutes, she stood up and began laying money on my desk. She said God had instructed her to give the money she had vowed . . . to me. That got my attention. So, I stood up and prayed with her. When we had finished praying, she said the amount she was giving me now was $200, but that was not all, and she would bring the rest later. We talked a few more minutes, and I asked her how much more money she was going to bring me. She said $800. You can imagine how excited I was. Three weeks from the time I had planted a $10-seed, I received $1,000 to purchase the computer for the young lady. Hallelujah! If you can believe all things are possible, (Mark 9:23) God will perform His Word. It takes only your obedience to sow your seed, and you will receive your harvest.

I have a big harvest coming. It's there. I just feel an excitement for what God's doing in my life. Because I have sown good seed, I can now reap a good harvest . . . and you can do the same. Always remember that when you have been obedient, you have a right to your reward. *You Decide Your Future By The Seeds You Sow.*

Notes

Make Your Decision

The Bible says in Romans 3:23, "For all have sinned, and come short of the glory of God." No one can enter the Kingdom of Heaven by their own efforts. Eternal security can only be possible by believing God's Word. Romans 10:9 says, "That if thou shalt confess with thy mouth the Lord Jesus and shalt believe in thine heart that God hath raised him from the dead, Thou shalt be saved."

To receive Jesus as your Lord and Savior, please pray this prayer in faith now.

"Dear Jesus, I confess with my mouth that you are Lord. I believe in my heart that you died for me, and that you rose again on the third day. Come into my life and forgive me of my sins. I receive you now as my Savior and Lord. Confirm your acceptance of me by giving me peace, joy and an uncommon love for others. Thank You for your love and forgiveness. Amen."

My Decision

Yes, Thomas, I have decided my future by accepting Jesus Christ as my personal Savior and Lord. Please send me more information to help me with my new life in Christ.

Name_____

Address_____

City_____ State_____

Zip_____ Phone_____

Birthday_____ E-Mail_____

Mail form to:

Thomas Meares

P. O. Box 2745

Lumberton, NC 28359

Website:

www.thomasmeares.com